_L.'B_

W9-ANF-522

PROPERTY OF
MOHONK PRESERVE, INC.

4'B

Illustrated
Facts & Records Book of
ANIMALS

Illustrated
Facts & Records Book of
ANIMALS

Theodore Rowland-Entwistle
Consultant: Michael Chinery

ARCO PUBLISHING, INC.
New York

Acknowledgements

Heather Angel: pages 11, 60T, 67, 68, 78T, 83, 88, 93, 118, Cover BR & BC.
Associated Press: page 21.
Australia News & Information Service: pages 109, 110T, 116B, 122B, 137.
J. Allan Cash: page 110B.
Michael Chinery: Cover BL.
Bruce Coleman: page 26/27, 69, 171, 185.
John Doidge: page 128.
Fishing News: page 73T.
Sonia Halliday: pages 167, 184T.
Eric & David Hosking: page 97.
Imitor: page 20.
E.D. Lacey: page 175B.
Mansell: page 32.
Micro Colour: page 29.
Pat Morris: pages 5, 12T & B, 13, 16, 17, 37, 38B, 41, 43C, 62BR, 63, 72B, 73B, 79T & B, 86, 117, 119B, 120T & B, 122T, 123, 130, 138, 139, 142, 143, 154, 155T & B, 157, 159, 160. 166T, 172, 174B, 181B, 186B, 222, Cover TC.
Natural History Photographic Agency: pages 5, 6T & B, 9TR, 24, 43T, 49, 50, 56, 62BL, 75, 78B, 84, 89, 99, 101, 102T & B, 104, 107, 111T, 115, 124T, 136, 140, 144, 150, 151T, 166B, 177, 179, 181T, 191, 197, 198, 199, 205, 215B.
Natural Science Photos: pages 6C, 39T, 45, 55L, 72T, 74, 87, 90R & L, 98, 116T, 119T, 146, 162, 168, 173, 175T, 176B, 183T & B, 188, 200, 203, 229.
New Zealand House: page 85.
Novosti Press: page 23.
Paul Popper: page 92.
Primate Research Laboratory, University of Wisconsin: page 219.
Satour: pages 9TL, 174T.
Seaphot: page 35.
Shell Ltd: page 53.
Survival: 133.
U.S. Navy: page 151B.
Zambia Tourist Office: pages 152/153.
Zefa: pages 163, 179.
Zoological Society: pages 8, 33, 125, 131, 140, 189, 217, 218.

Published 1983 by Arco Publishing, Inc. 215 Park Avenue South, New York, N.Y. 10003. © Grisewood & Dempsey Ltd. 1981.

Printed in Hong Kong by South China Printing Co.

Library of Congress Catalog Card No. 82–18406.

ISBN 0-668-05730-0

Contents

EVOLUTION

Two hundred years ago Christians firmly believed the Bible story of the Creation as told in Genesis was literally true. Today it is generally accepted that simple organisms gradually evolved (developed) into more complicated ones—a process that took place over thousands of generations and which is still going on. This is the *theory of evolution,* which caused a dreadful storm when the naturalists Charles Darwin and Alfred Russel Wallace put it forward in 1858.

When the Earth was first formed some 4,500 million years ago its atmosphere did not contain enough oxygen to support life. Geologists believe that oxygen first appeared in any quantity in the form of water, which forms 97 per cent of the gaseous discharge of every volcano. Water molecules were broken up into oxygen and hydrogen by the action of ultra-violet light from the Sun.

In time ozone—a form of oxygen—formed a barrier in the atmosphere which screened the Sun's ultra-violet rays, which are harmful to life. At some stage after that life must have begun spontaneously. It would have started when carbon, the essential element in all living things, combined with other elements. Among the compounds thus formed would be amino acids, the building blocks of life. They are made up of carbon, nitrogen, hydrogen, and oxygen. From such compounds, life evolved.

A giant tortoise from the Galapagos Islands. Darwin observed how the shells of Galapagos tortoises vary in shape from one island to another. Such evidence of variation and change helped him to develop his theory of evolution.

Animals have lived on Earth for at least 700 million years. Their remains have been preserved in the soil and rocks as fossils, and from these fossils it has been possible to reconstruct what the animals looked like.

THE FOSSIL RECORD

Fossils show that the first animals were invertebrates that lived in the seas around 700 million years ago. The first vertebrates appeared about 500 million years ago, and were like armoured fish. Fish with lungs which could use their fins as legs developed nearly 400 million years ago. The first land vertebrates were amphibians which flourished some 50 million years later. About the same time came the first insects, spiders, and scorpions—including dragonflies with 2-foot (60-cm) wingspans. They were followed by the first reptiles. The age of the dinosaurs, the giant reptiles, lasted from 225 million to 65 million years ago, when the mammals took over. We are still in the mammal age.

Above: The body of a spider preserved almost intact in amber — the hardened resin of pine trees.

Fossil ammonites, ancient shellfish (cephalopods) whose shells were often tightly coiled.

There are three main kinds of fossils.

Mould fossils were made when an animal was trapped in mud or clay which hardened around it. When the substance of the animal's body disintegrated, it left a hollow in the stone which formed from the mud.

Print fossils were made in a similar way, when mud, bearing the print of an animal's foot or its body, hardened and turned to rock.

Petrified fossils were formed when the body materials were dissolved slowly by the action of water. Minerals in the water were deposited to take the place of the material, in the same way as stalactites or stalagmites are formed in a cave. Petrified fossils are mostly of bones or shells, because the soft parts of the body dissolve very quickly.

A fossil coelacanth, a lobe-finned fish of Devonian times. These fish had fins they could use as legs. From their relatives evolved the first land vertebrates — the amphibians.

FOSSIL RECORDS

Oldest fossil of an animal is of a clamlike creature that lived more than 720 million years ago. It was found on Victoria Island, in Canada's Northwest Territories.

Earliest fossil egg is about 250 million years old, and is of a kind of reptile. It was found in Texas.

Largest fossil remains are those of *Brachiosaurus*, a 50-tonne dinosaur. They were found in East Africa and North America.

Earliest fossil land animals were amphibians that lived just over 350 million years ago. They were found in Greenland.

The Age of Dinosaurs

Turtles first evolved about 200 million years ago, and have changed little since. Proganochelys was about the size of a modern turtle. Neither of these ancient reptiles were dinosaurs, but their descendents have out-lived the dinosaurs.

For over 150 million years the Earth was dominated by some of the most extraordinary creatures that ever walked—the giant reptiles, popularly known as the dinosaurs. The age of the dinosaurs was the Mesozoic Era, which lasted from about 225 million years ago to 65 million years ago. The term 'dinosaur' was coined in 1842 by the English zoologist Richard Owen, from two Greek words meaning 'monstrous lizard'. Dinosaurs are not in fact one group, but two, and they were not lizards. Most of the giant reptiles were vegetarians, but the few flesh-eaters were indeed terrible. Some walked on two feet, others on four. But from having been the lords of the Earth, the dinosaurs died out, leaving the world to the mammals.

Below: Protosuchus was one of the direct ancestors of the crocodiles.

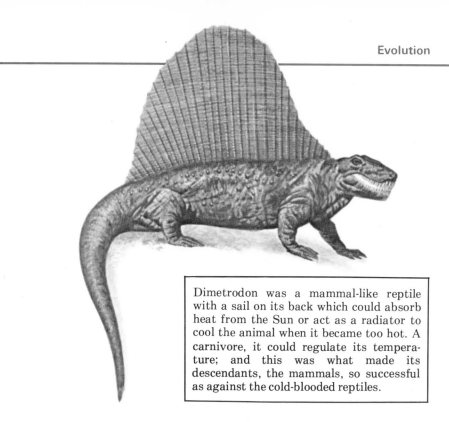

Dimetrodon was a mammal-like reptile with a sail on its back which could absorb heat from the Sun or act as a radiator to cool the animal when it became too hot. A carnivore, it could regulate its temperature; and this was what made its descendants, the mammals, so successful as against the cold-blooded reptiles.

Hylonomous is probably the oldest known reptile. It was an insect-eater, about 4 feet (1.4 m) long, and lived about 320 million years ago. It survived about 50 million years, but died out as the giant reptiles took over.

THE TYRANT REPTILE

The most terrible of all the 'terrible lizards' was undoubtedly *Tyrannosaurus*, the 'tyrant' reptile. At about 50 feet (15 m) long and 19 feet (6m) tall, it was the largest flesh-eating animal that ever stalked the Earth. *Tyrannosaurus* was a biped, walking erect on its powerful hind legs, and balancing with its tail like a monstrous kangaroo. Its front legs were so short they could not even reach the creature's mouth. Each of its 'attenuated' hands had just two feeble fingers on it. But the *Tyrannosaurus* skull was a massive, 4-foot (1.2-m) long structure, and its mouth was filled with sharp teeth for rending its prey's flesh.

Fossilized dinosaur eggs, examples of cast or mould fossils. Mineral matter has completely replaced the original material and no trace of the original internal structure can be seen.

Right: Footprints of a giant — the fossilized tracks of a Hadrosaur, a herbivorous dinosaur, found in British Columbia, Canada.

The official zoological name for the giant reptiles is *Archosauria*, or ruling lizards. They are divided into two orders.

The Saurischia were the lizard-hipped dinosaurs, so-called from the very distinctive arrangement of their hip bones, which resembled that of today's lizards. They were subdivided into two groups, the *sauropods*, which ate vegetation, and the *theropods*, which ate flesh.

The Ornithiscia were the bird-hipped dinosaurs, whose hip skeltons bore some resemblances to those of present-day birds. They were divided into four groups: *ornithopods*, which walked on two legs and included some with bills like a duck's; *stegosaurs*, which had great bony plates for protection; *ankylosaurs*, which were even more heavily armoured; and *ceratopians*, or horned dinosaurs.

WHAT KILLED THE DINOSAURS?

The end of the dinosaurs has always been a riddle for palaeontologists. The fossil record shows that these great beasts disappeared after a rapid decline about 65 million years ago. Several theories have been put forward to explain this.

One theory suggests that the dinosaurs were killed off by climatic changes which

Chart showing how the early groups of reptiles evolved.

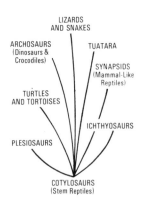

LIZARDS AND SNAKES

ARCHOSAURS (Dinosaurs & Crocodiles)

TUATARA

SYNAPSIDS (Mammal-Like Reptiles)

TURTLES AND TORTOISES

ICHTHYOSAURS

PLESIOSAURS

COTYLOSAURS (Stem Reptiles)

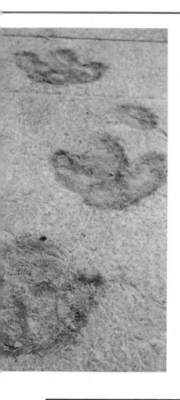

occurred at this time. Another theory suggests that the development of egg-eating mammals may have been the chief cause. Some scientists even think that certain harmful bacteria may have evolved at this time and wiped out most of the large reptiles, though there is as yet very little evidence to support this.

One of the richest deposits of dinosaur skeletons and fossils lies in the United States, in the adjoining northern corners of Utah and Colorado. It has been preserved as a Dinosaur National Monument.

REPTILE RECORDS

Largest dinosaur was *Brachiosaurus,* a plant-eating animal that grew more than 80 feet (24m) long, and weighed about 50 tonnes. Its neck reached upwards to a height from the ground of 40 feet (12m), and it could easily have looked over a three-storey building.

Longest dinosaur was *Diplodocus,* a comparatively slender animal almost 90 feet (27 m) long.

Smallest dinosaur was *Compsognathus,* which was about the size of a large present-day chicken. Including its long tail it was only 2½ feet (75 cm) long.

Largest flying reptile was *Pteranodon,* one specimen of which had a wingspan of 27 feet (8 m). In March 1975 the discovery of the remains of a reptile with a wing-span of about 50 feet (15 m) was reported.

Archaeopteryx

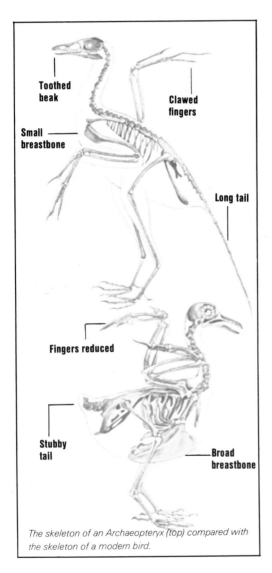

Toothed beak

Clawed fingers

Small breastbone

Long tail

Fingers reduced

Stubby tail

Broad breastbone

The skeleton of an Archaeopteryx (top) compared with the skeleton of a modern bird.

Below: The crow-sized Archaeopteryx was half reptile and half bird. Its tail was still long and bony, like a lizard's, but a row of feathers down each side made gliding and steering easier. Its wings were weak and had claws for climbing trees. It had small, sharp teeth and scales on its face and head, although the rest of its body was covered with feathers.

The lucky discovery of an *Archaeopteryx* fossil in 1861 revealed the missing link between reptiles and birds. The skeleton resembled that of a small gliding reptile. What distinguished it as a bird, however, were the faint but clear imprints of its feathers. *Archaeopteryx* was not a strong flier but its long tail was rimmed with feathers that helped it steer and glide. It is likely that it was also a warm-blooded animal and therefore would have been more active than any reptile.

Because bird skeletons are light and fragile they are rarely preserved as fossils. The early birds were probably forest-dwellers. When they died their bodies would have fallen to the ground and been destroyed by other animals. It is only when birds became strong fliers that they left behind any evidence of themselves.

Rise of the Mammals

Mammals already existed at the time of the early dinosaurs, 160 million years ago. Throughout the Age of the Dinosaurs, which lasted until 65 million years ago, all mammals were small, inconspicuous, hairy creatures. The earliest mammals laid eggs like reptiles, and also like the platypus and echidna of today.

About 100 million years ago, the first marsupials appeared. These are mammals in a more familiar sense, since they do not lay eggs but give birth to live, active young. But the newborn marsupial is at a much less developed stage of life than, say, a newborn kitten or human being. For example, a kangaroo at birth is less than an inch (two centimetres) long, without developed eyes and ears, and quite hairless.

After the dinosaurs had died out, mammals rapidly increased in size, number and variety, to fill all the ecological niches that the great reptiles had occupied. By this time, modern, or placental, mammals had appeared. Unlike

A reconstruction of Arsinotherium. It was the size of a rhinoceros and lived in marshes. It had two pairs of horns, one large and one small. There is no fossil record of its ancestors or descendants.

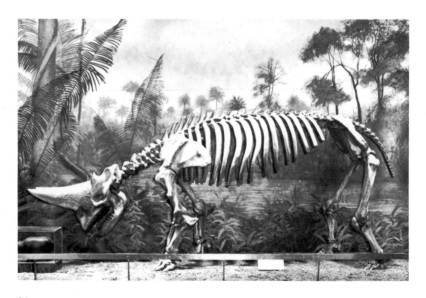

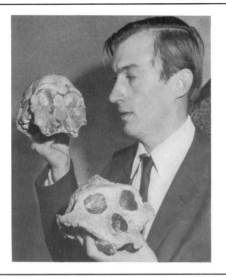

Richard Leakey, the anthropologist, compares the cast of a skull $2\frac{1}{2}$ million years old (top) with that of a million-year-old Australopithecus.

marsupials, these mammals are born at a fairly advanced stage of development, having been nourished while inside their mothers, through a feeding and respiratory organ called the placenta. A few parts of the world, however, continued to house a largely marsupial mammal fauna. These included South America and Australia — island continents that first broke away from the ancient supercontinent of Pangaea. Australia which still remains an isolated island continent, continues to have a largely marsupial fauna.

PREHISTORIC RECORD
Largest land mammal ever known was a hornless rhinoceros, Baluchitherium, which roamed parts of Asia about 40,000,000 years ago. It was about 27 feet (8 m) long, stood 17 feet (5 m) high at the shoulders, and had a skull 5 feet (1.5 m) long.

ARE MAMMOTHS EXTINCT?
Mammoths were large, woolly animals similar to elephants. They are frequently portrayed in Stone Age cave paintings in southern Europe, so they were known between 10,000 and 20,000 years ago. Not only skeletons but completely frozen carcases have been found trapped in the glaciers of Siberia.

Because of the location of the frozen specimens, people assumed the mammoth was an Arctic animal. But the contents of the stomachs of some mammoths show that they fed on forest plants—so the mammoth may have been an animal of warmer climates. It is even possible that some mammoths still survive in the *taiga*, a vast area of coniferous forest in northern Asia. Local hunters have often reported seeing animals that from their descriptions sound very like mammoths!

A mammoth found almost intact in Siberia, now stuffed and preserved in a museum. Not even its long, coarse hair decayed.

WHY MANY ANIMALS DIED OUT

Man himself has been responsible for the end of many species in historical times, but the numbers that have become extinct in that time are as nothing compared with the numbers that have died out in previous eras. Undoubtedly the Ice Ages created conditions in which animals could not survive. Even so that would not account for all the changes.

Continental drift may very well be one answer. A hundred million years ago the continents were not in their present positions—that is why Alaska, a land of snow and ice, has rich deposits of oil and natural gas that could only have formed in a tropical climate. Since it is unlikely that tropical conditions could ever have existed so close to the North Pole, then Alaska itself must have moved.

The American bison almost became extinct in the late 19th century, when only 550 remained. In 1889 it was protected from hunting by law, and now about 10,000 live in the United States alone.

Some animal species— 'living fossils'—have lived on, almost unchanged, for millions of years after their close relations died out. The horseshoe crab (1) is an arachnid that has survived

for 200 million years. (2) The coelacanth, thought to have died out 70 million years ago, was found alive and swimming in 1938. The ancestors of peripatus (3) left their traces in rocks 500 million years ago. (4) The okapi, unchanged for 30 million years. Its only relative is the giraffe. Lingula (5), one of the brachiopods, has a longer history than any other genus—over 500 million years. (6) The Australian lungfish, as ancient as the coelacanth. The tuatara (7), closely related to the dinosaurs, has not changed since then.

ANIMAL KINGDOM

Plants and animals are classified in two groups or kingdoms, the **Animal kingdom** and the **Plant kingdom**. Most plants have the ability to manufacture their own food from air, water, and minerals in the soil, and they get their power to do this from the Sun.

Animals can not manufacture their basic food. They eat plants, or other animals that feed on plants. Most animals can move about, too. So it is relatively easy to tell plants from animals, until you come to the very tiny, one-celled creatures such as bacteria. Some scientists think that these creatures should form a third kingdom, that of the protists.

There are about one million kinds of animals, ranging from the giant Blue whale to the microscopic protozoans. The insects form the largest group. Scientists have so far identified about 700,000 different kinds. Mammals, the group that includes dogs, cats, horses — and Man — total around 4,000 species. Other species' totals include birds: 11,000; reptiles: 5,000; fishes: 13,000; amphibians: 3,000; centipedes: 2,000 and millipedes: 8,000. Arachnids — the spiders and their allies — tot up an amazing 35,000 species.

Lionesses at rest between hunting bouts. They are the providers for the lion troupe. Male lions do little hunting until they are old and solitary; however, the males of a troupe generally get the choicest pickings.

LARGEST, SMALLEST, FASTEST, OLDEST

Largest animal is the Blue or Sulphur-bottom whale (*Balaenoptera musculus*). Specimens have been caught measuring more than 100 feet (30 m) long, though Blue whales this size have not been seen for many years.

Smallest animals are some of the protozoa, single-celled creatures. Many of them are around 2μ (0.00007874 in) long. They can be seen only with a powerful microscope.

Largest animal living on land is the African elephant (*Loxodonta africana*). Bull elephants are about 11½ feet (3.5 m) tall and weigh up to 7 tonnes.

Longest living animal is the Giant tortoise (*Testudo elephantopus*), known to live up to 177 years.

Fastest animal on land is the cheetah (*Acinonyx jubatus*), which can run at up to 65 mph (105 kph) over short distances.

Fastest fliers are probably Common swifts which can reach 100 mph (160 kph) in level flight; peregrine falcons (*Falco peregrinus*) can dive at up to 180 mph (290 kph).

Greatest traveller is the Arctic tern (*Sterna paradisaea*) which migrates every year from the Arctic to the Antarctic and back, a round trip of 22,000 miles (36,000 km).

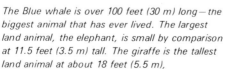

The Blue whale is over 100 feet (30 m) long — the biggest animal that has ever lived. The largest land animal, the elephant, is small by comparison at 11.5 feet (3.5 m) tall. The giraffe is the tallest land animal at about 18 feet (5.5 m),

The peregrine falcon — the
fastest moving bird as it
dives at 180 mph (290 kph).
Fastest flying birds are the
swifts which can reach 100
mph (160 kph) in level
flight.

Tiny paramecia, one of
the smallest forms of animal
life, can hardly be seen with
the naked eye.

29

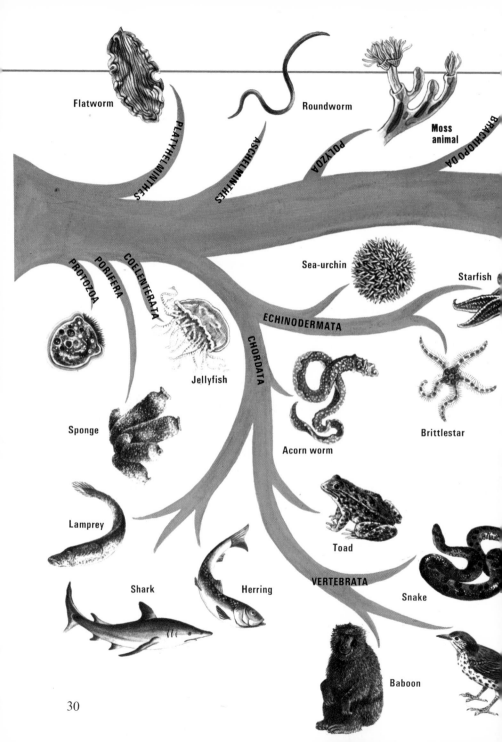

Flatworm

PLATYHELMINTHES

Roundworm

ASCHELMINTHES

POLYZOA

Moss animal

BRACHIOPODA

Sea-urchin

Starfish

ECHINODERMATA

PROTOZOA

PORIFERA

COELENTERATA

CHORDATA

Jellyfish

Brittlestar

Sponge

Acorn worm

Lamprey

Toad

Shark

Herring

VERTEBRATA

Snake

Baboon

30

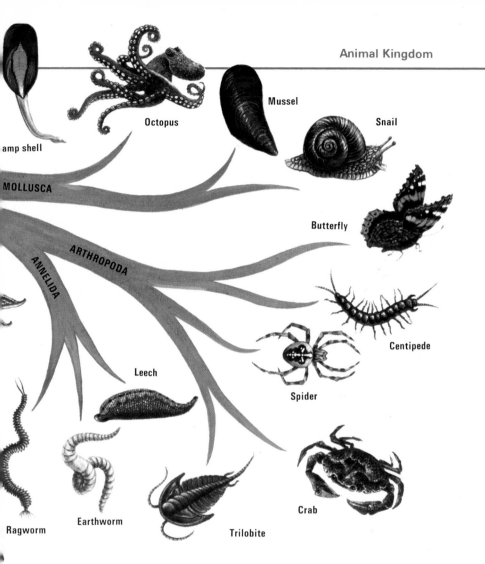

Mussel

Snail

Octopus

amp shell

MOLLUSCA

Butterfly

ARTHROPODA

ANNELIDA

Centipede

Leech

Spider

Crab

Ragworm

Earthworm

Trilobite

Thrush

The tree on the left shows the main groups in the animal kingdom. The smallest branches represent classes (for example, the baboon, a mammal). Some of the classes of worms and other small groups have been omitted.

Scientists recognize three main groups of animals. **Protozoa** are single-celled animals. **Parazoa** (sponges) have many cells, but are not closely related to the **Metazoa,** which constitute the vast majority of many-celled animals. The most sophisticated of the Metazoa are the Chordates — animals with a rod-like structure to support the body.

31

Classification

The Latin names used in classification relate either to the type of animal, or in some cases to the person who discovered it, or the place where it flourishes. The genus name is always printed with a capital letter, and the species name with a small letter. If a proper name is used in a species, it is always Latinized, as for example in the name of Coke's hartebeeste, *Alcephalus cokei.*

Karl von Linné, the Swede who founded the modern system of classification of plants and animals and gave them Latin names. He even latinized his own name to Carolus Linnaeus.

Zoologists use Latin names for describing animals in order to be quite sure what animal they are talking about. Names for animals differ widely from one language to another. For example, the English *bear* is the Italian *orso,* the French *ours,* and the German *Bär.* But all nations can understand clearly what is meant by the family name for bears, Ursidae.

Another reason for having an international Latin 'code' is that the same name often describes different animals, even in the same language. For example, to Englishmen a robin is a small songbird, *Erithacus rubecula.* An American would be referring to a larger bird of the same family, *Turdus migratorius,* while to an Australian a robin is a kind of fly-catcher, genus *Petroica.* Americans generally call bison (genus *Bison*) buffalo, while in the Old World a buffalo is any one of several animals similar to an ox. Just to add to the confusion, the jack rabbit (*Lepus californicus*) of North America is really a hare!

In *taxonomy*—the science of classification —there are seven basic ranks, which to a zoologist explain exactly what kind of animal he is reading about. There are also a number of intermediate ranks.

Kingdom is the highest rank. An organism can belong to either the Plantae or the Animalia kingdom—though some scientists make a claim for a third kingdom, the Protista, for organisms on the borderline, such as bacteria.

Phylum (plural phyla) is the largest sub-division of the animal kingdom, covering animals of broadly similar character. For example, all animals with any kind of backbone are in the phylum Chordata.

Class, the main sub-division of a phylum, brings together animals with a closer relationship. The class Mammalia, for instance, embraces all animals that suckle their young and have mammary glands.

Order takes the sub-division a stage farther. The Mammalia, for example, are divided into 18 orders, such as the Marsupialia, Primates, Rodentia, and Carnivora.

Family includes animals that are recognizably similar. Among the Carnivora, the flesh-eaters, the family Felidae includes all the cat-like animals.

Genus (plural genera) is a group of closely related animals within a family. The Felidae include the genera *Panthera*—the big cats such as lions; *Felis*—cats that purr but do not roar; *Acinonyx*—the cheetah with its non-retractible claws; and *Lynx*—the lynx.

Species is the smallest division, and defines animals that are of the same kind and that can breed together. Lions *(Panthera leo)* and tigers *(Panthera tigris)* are two species in the genus *Panthera*. Occasionally different species will mate; in captivity lions and tigers interbreed, producing ligers where the father is a lion, and tigons where the father is a tiger. The offspring, however, are sterile; they cannot reproduce.

Systems
Since the use of Latin names for classification began in the 18th century, there have been many alterations. Even now scientists are re-writing lists in the light of greater modern knowledge. American and European classifications are not always identical. But today scientists are tending to adopt the rulings of the International Code of Zoological Nomenclature (ICZN). An international commission meets to resolve disputes.

The American Timber wolf and the European wolf are both varieties of the same animal. They differ only in colour and size—just as members of the human race do. A complete classification of the animal is as follows:

Kingdom: *Animalia*
  Phylum: *Chordata*
    Subphylum: *Vertebrata*
      Class: *Mammalia*
        Order: *Carnivora*
          Family: *Canidae*
            Genus: *Canis*
              Species: *lupus*

INVERTE-BRATES

Invertebrates are animals without backbones. Usually they do not have any form of internal skeleton, although some, like the cuttlefish, have internal shells. They range from the single-celled protozoans to insects, worms, snails and oysters.

Simple Creatures

All living creatures are made up of cells, little units of life. The very simplest animals consist of single cells. They are called Protozoa, which means 'first animals', and the earliest forms of animal life must have been of this kind. Scientists do not know how many species there are. At least 30,000 have been identified, and several times as many have not yet been classified. It is quite impossible to estimate how many individuals there are—millions upon millions, far more than any other kind of animal life.

Scientists do not agree on how to classify these tiny creatures. But there are four basic kinds, grouped according to how they move about. Almost all live in water.

Flagellates have long whip-like threads (flagella) that thrash about to drive them through the water.

Sarcodines are creatures that move by putting out a part of the cell wall to form what is called a pseudopod—literally 'false foot'. The rest of the cell then moves into it.

Life in a rock pool. The brightly coloured invertebrate sea animals include a starfish, a sea urchin and several sea anemones. The white spiral object is a fish's egg case.

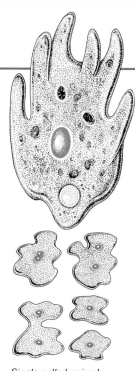

Sporozoans are parasites, very tiny, with no particular locomotion.

Ciliates have fine hair-like structures, or cilia, which they use to move with and to capture their food.

A DIVERSITY OF CREATURES

Single-celled animals vary as much as larger and more complicated ones in their bodies and their ways of life.

The amoeba is one of the best known. This completely shapeless animal is made of a soft lump of protoplasm—the basic building material of which living things are made. It moves by pushing out pseudopods and then 'flowing' into them. It catches its prey the same way, surrounding it by pseudopods and then digesting it. An amoeba reproduces asexually by fission (splitting apart). The nucleus divides first and the rest of the amoeba follows.

Difflugia is a relative of the amoeba which lives in ponds. It builds itself a house out of sand grains, with its pseudopods projecting from one end.

Heliozoans are tiny pond animals that grow a kind of external skeleton for support. The name means 'sun animal', and comes because the long and stiff pseudopods project through the skeleton like the Sun's rays.

Single-celled animals are the simplest of all creatures. The amoeba is a blob of protoplasm surrounding a central nucleus. It reproduces by splitting—first the nucleus divides and then the cell splits apart.

PROTOZOAN RECORDS

Smallest protozoans are some red-blood-cell parasites, which measure only 2μ (0.00007874 in) long. One red blood cell can hold at least 10—and there are about 5 million red blood cells in each cubic millimetre of blood.

Largest protozoans may be up to 0.197 in (5 mm) long, and some have been reported longer still.

Most beautiful protozoans are the radiolarians, which have elaborate shells. Few of them can be seen without a hand-lens.

Sponges

When you wash your back with a sponge you are using the skeleton of one of the simplest kinds of many-celled animals. The sponge had scientists baffled for many years because it does not move about like an animal, but stays anchored to one spot in the sea, like a plant. Sponges grow in a variety of shapes, some of them remarkably plant-like—though a bath sponge when lifted out of the water looks more like a lump of liver than anything else.

A typical sponge is a mass of cup-like organs riddled with holes and pores. The animal lives by drawing water in through the pores, filtering out any food it may contain, and pumping it out through the larger holes. The water is pumped by large numbers of flagella which literally whip the water and make it move.

Some sponges reproduce sexually, by producing eggs and sperms. Others reproduce by producing buds and branches, rather like plants. Most sponges live in the sea, and the bath sponge (*Euspongia*) grows in warm, shallow water.

The glassy skeleton of the Venus flower basket sponge. The living sponge is covered by a thin, delicate layer of flesh.

SPONGE RECORDS

Greatest depth at which sponges have been found living is more than 28,000 feet (8,500 m).

Greatest altitude at which freshwater sponges have been found is in crater lakes 10,000 feet (3,000 m) above sea level.

Oldest fossil sponges lived more than 600,000,000 years ago in Pre-Cambrian times.

Largest sponges are of many shapes and sizes. Some are up to 9 feet (2.7 m) long; others are more than 6 feet 6 inches (2 m) across.

Smallest sponges consist of single cups a few millimetres high, but they usually grow together in colonies.

Echinoderms

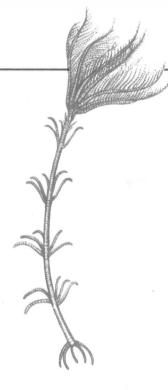

Echinoderms, or spiny-skinned animals, is a great group or phylum that is not related very obviously to any other invertebrate group. Although not at all closely related to the coelenterates, they have one important thing in common with them. Both these kinds of animals have radial, or wheel-spoke symmetry, unlike most other groups of animals, which are either asymmetrical or, like mammals, have bilateral symmetry, in which the left half of the body is a mirror image of the right half.

Echinoderms fall into five well-defined groups: starfishes, sea urchins, sea cucumbers, sea lilies and brittle stars. Although they look so different from one another, they are all built on the same radial plan.

Despite its name and appearance, the sea-lily is an animal.

Three types of echinoderm, all common creatures of coastal waters.

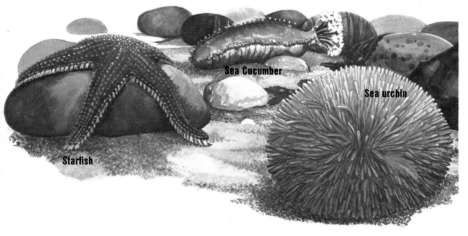

Sea Cucumber

Sea urchin

Starfish

Coelenterates

The coelenterates, also known as cnidarians, are the third simplest form of life, coming after the protozoa and sponges. Their bodies consist of a double layer of cells, with a jelly-like substance, sometimes mixed with cells, in between. A mouth leads to the large digestive cavity. The animals have nervous systems, but no heads as such. A most striking feature of the coelenterates is their radial symmetry, their bodies being built on a plan resembling the spokes of a wheel. There are three major groups:

Hydrozoa include more than 2,700 species. One type, the sea fir, looks more like a plant than an animal. Sea hair (*Sertularia*) is a type that is dried and stained to be used as a decorative material.

Scyphozoa are large jellyfish. Most of them swim freely in the sea. The common jellyfish (*Aurelia aurita*) is typical of many in that buds from the adult attach themselves to a rock and develop into a form known as a scyphistoma. This produces larvae which in turn develop into adult jellyfish.

Anthozoa include corals, sea-anemones, and other ornamental forms.

The sea-anemone looks like a plant. Its tentacles sting the prey and carry it to the mouth which they surround.

A colony of coral is made up of the hard skeletons of thousands of polyps.

JELLYFISH

Although its name makes it sound feeble and inoffensive, the jellyfish is a carnivore, an eater of other animal life. It is one of a group of sea creatures—and a few freshwater ones —which are slightly more complex than sponges. These creatures are called coelenterates, from the hollow gut or digestive system with which they are equipped, a *coelenteron.*

Coelenterates vary greatly. Some, like the jellyfish, have soft bodies and long tentacles. Others, like the corals, have chalky skeletons. Some move about, others stay in one place. Coelenterates include some of the most beautiful of sea creatures, which look like fans, ferns, and flowers.

When it comes to reproduction, many coelenterates show what is called the alternation of generations. In one generation the animal reproduces sexually, with male and female cells. The next generation reproduces asexually, by budding. The sexual stage is a free-swimming form, called a medusa. The asexual stage is a polyp, a cylindrical animal anchored to a rock at one end with an open mouth at the other.

DANGER AT SEA

Despite their beautiful and innocent appearance, many coelenterates are dangerous. They sting their prey, and the sting of some of these animals is enough to kill a man. The Portuguese man o' war (*Physalia physalis*) belongs to a group known as Siphonophores. The creature is actually a colony of polyps and medusae, buoyed up by a float which looks like a blue or pink plastic bag, up to 12 inches (30 cm) long. The polyps and their tentacles feel like red-hot pins and can paralyse a fish. Unfortunately, even when jellyfish are broken up into pieces along sea-shores, their sting remains active and can be painful or irritating to bathers.

Left: The Portuguese man o' war is a colony of polyps that floats on the surface of the sea. It has tentacles up to 35 feet (10.5 m) long, lined with stinging cells whose poison is as powerful as that of the cobra.

One relation of the Portuguese man o' war actually hoists a sail and is driven along by the wind.

Its float is flat and oval, with a vertical sail inflated by gas. The sail is set at an angle to the 'keel' of the animal. Some have it set from right to left; others from left to right, so that they take different courses.

THE WORLD OF CORALS

Full fathom five thy father lies.
Of his bones are coral made,

wrote Shakespeare. Although coral is not the bones of shipwrecked sailors, it is a skeleton—that of millions of tiny polyps. The coral polyp attaches itself to a rock under the sea. As a protection for its soft body it builds a skeleton around the lower part, using limestone which it filters from the seawater around it. When it dies the skeleton remains.

Reefs and atolls have been built up over the centuries by skeletons of countless millions of such coral polyps. They are found only in warm seas, since the vast colonies of corals that form them flourish only in sea temperatures over 65°F (18°C). Reefs form on shallow continental shelves, close to the shore. The biggest is the Great Barrier Reef off the eastern coast of Australia. It is 1,250 miles (2,000 km) long. Atolls are ring-shaped islands, built up on the submerged tops of extinct volcanoes.

Corals come in an amazing variety—some are like shrubs or gnarled branches, some look like the underside of edible mushrooms and some are like intricate mazes.

COELENTERATE RECORDS

Smallest coelenterates are tiny polyp forms about one twenty-fifth of an inch (1mm) long. The **smallest medusae** are about one-sixteenth of an inch (1.5mm) across.

Largest coelenterates are the medusa forms of the jellyfish *Cyanea arctica*, which have bells more than six feet (1.8m) across, with tentacles up to 120 feet (36m) long.

Most valuable forms of coral are the red coral (*Corallium rubrum*) of the Mediterranean Sea, and the jet black kind, known as king's coral, found in the Indian Ocean.

Worms

Not all worms are long and wriggly. The bristleworms (class Polychaeta) include many strange and beautiful creatures. The sea mouse (*Aphrodite aculeata*) is a broad oval animal, covered with fine bristles which look like fur. This coat is irridescent, appearing green, blue, red, or yellow as the angle of the light changes. Another family of bristleworms, the featherdusters (Sabellidae), have long feathery tentacles at one end. They live on the sea-shore, inside long tubes made of grains of sand.

Below: If a turbellarian or free-living flatworm is deprived of food for a long time, it will begin to eat itself. The missing organs can be regrown when it feeds normally. If the worm is cut into pieces each will grow into a complete worm.

The name 'worm' covers a great variety of animals, which have little in common but their long, thin shape. The grubs or larvae of some insects look worm-like, but are not worms. True worms range in size from microscopic forms to 60-foot (18 m) tapeworms. Many are parasites on larger animals, including Man.

Worms differ from each other much more than might be supposed; they are not even all in the same phylum or major group.

Platyhelminthes are the most primitive kind of worm. They have no blood system to carry nutriments, but their digestive system spreads around to carry food direct to various parts of the body. This phylum of flatworms includes planarians (most of which live in water), flukes, and tapeworms. There are about 5,500 species.

Nemertina (also called **Rhynchocoaela**), the ribbonworms, are long, flat creatures whose heads contain a harpoon-like structure which can be shot out to catch other small creatures for food.

Annelida is the group of segmented worms. They are the most advanced of worms, and include earthworms, bristleworms, and leeches.

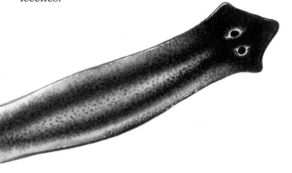

Largest tapeworm is probably the human tapeworm, *Diphyllobothrium latum*, which may be 60 feet (18 m) long. Specimens of 30 feet (9 m) are common.

Longest ribbonworms may grow up to 90 feet (27 m) long, though most species are less than 7 feet (2 m).

Longest worm found in Britain is the Bootlace worm (*Lineus longissimus*). One specimen was 33 feet (10 m) long when fully unravelled. It is difficult to measure because it coils up.

Above: A lugworm and its cast. Lugworms make their burrows by eating their way through the sand, digesting any nourishing matter and casting the rest out in a coil on the surface.

Right: The peacock worm, a marine bristleworm, lives in long tubes of sand. Food is filtered from the water by tentacles, and passes down them to a central mouth. Some of these creatures have reactions up to 100 times faster than Man's.

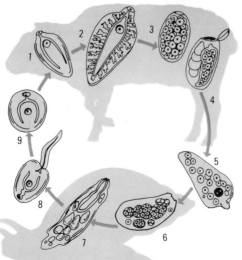

The liver fluke is a tiny parasitic flatworm. The liver fluke in the illustration has two hosts, a sheep and a snail. The sheep eats the cyst (1) which turns into an adult fluke (2). This lays eggs (3) in the liver, which ripen (4), are excreted, and produce a miracidium (5). This enters a water snail and turns into a sporocyst (6) containing rediae. These become second rediae (7) containing cercariae (8) which leave the snail, swim to the water's edge, and turn into cysts (9).

43

Molluscs

Molluscs are a group of animals with soft bodies, and they make up one of the largest phyla of the animal kingdom. To protect their soft bodies most molluscs have shells, like the snail or the oyster. But some, like the octopus, are completely unprotected.

There are more than 46,000 living species of molluscs, and many more fossil varieties. They are grouped in these six classes:

Right: The Giant clam is the largest of all bivalve molluscs.

Monoplacophora have simple, cap-shaped shells. Only three living species are known, though many fossils have been found. The first living specimen, genus *Neopilina*, was discovered 11,800 feet (3,590 m) down in the Pacific as recently as 1952.

Amphineura are simple sea creatures. Some are worm-like; others, such as the chitons, have shells made up of eight plates.

Gastropoda form the largest group, and include snails, slugs, and limpets.

Scaphopoda, or tusk shells, have long tube-like shells. They burrow in the sand and mud of the sea-bed, usually in deep water.

Pelecypoda or bivalves have shells made in two halves (called 'valves') hinged together. They include clams and oysters.

Cephalopoda is a class including squids, cuttlefishes, and octopuses—and some of the largest sea creatures as far as length goes.

All molluscs have a fairly well developed nervous system, and cephalopods have well developed brains, too. Most molluscs have a single broad-soled foot, on which the animal can crawl by a series of muscle contractions. Molluscs tend to move slowly, but octopuses and squids are fast swimmers. Many molluscs, such as oysters, swim about when they are young, then settle down to a quiet life on the sea floor.

The twin-shelled molluscs known as bivalves are remarkable in many ways—and one is that unlike most molluscs they have no heads. A thick fold of skin called the mantle lies inside the shell and it has sensitive edges. It may have tentacles, and in some species many eyes. Most bivalves live buried in mud or sand, filtering food from the water.

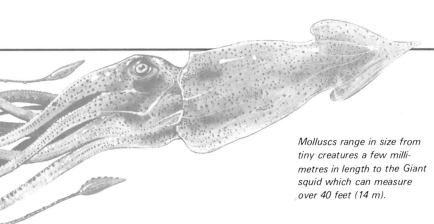

Molluscs range in size from tiny creatures a few milli-metres in length to the Giant squid which can measure over 40 feet (14 m).

THE AMAZING OCTOPUS

The Common octopus (*Octopus vulgaris*) is found in seas all over the world. It is so called because it has eight legs. It lives in rocks and crevices, looking out with its well-developed eyes for its prey. It particularly likes sea urchins, and small molluscs and crustaceans. It captures it prey in a sudden rush, and kills it with a bite.

The octopus's brain is well developed compared with those of other molluscs. The French underwater explorer Jacques-Yves Cousteau reported finding an octopus city under the sea. Evidently there was a shortage of natural holes, so some octopuses had built their own, propping up a large slab of rock on several smaller ones to form a lean-to roof and building a rubble wall in front.

GIANT MOLLUSCS

Largest bivalve is the Giant clam (genus *Tridacna*) found on coral reefs in the East Indies and Australia. The shells can be more than 4 feet (1.2 m) across and weigh more than 500 lb (230 kg).

Largest octopus is the common Pacific octopus (*Octopus hongkongensis*), which can measure up to 32 feet (9.7 m) from the tip of one tentacle to the tip of the opposite one.

Largest squid is the Giant squid (genus *Architeuthis*), which can have a body 13 feet (4 m) long with tentacles over 30 feet (9 m) long.

45

Invertebrates: animals without backbones

Phylum	Common name, if any	No. of species	Description and examples
Protozoa	Single-celled animals	More than 30,000	A great, various group of mostly micro-scopically small creatures having only one cell. They include *Amoeba*, which lives in mud, *Paramecium*, which swims in water, and *Plasmodium*, which lives in blood, causing malaria.
Mesozoa	none	About 50	Tiny animal parasites having only a few cells.
Porifera	Sponges	About 5,000	Many-celled animals, but with only a few kinds of cells. Live mostly in sea.
Coel-enterata	Jellyfish and relatives	About 9,500	Water animals in which the body is either a *medusa*, as in jellyfish, or a *polyp*, as in sea anemones, corals, and *Hydra*.
Ctenophora	Comb jellies	About 100	Similar to small jellyfish, but swim by beating of 'combs'.
Platy-helminthes	Flatworms	About 5,500	Worms with very flat bodies. Some swim about in water. Others (tape-worms and flukes) are parasites.
Nemertina	Ribbonworms	750	Sea worms rather like flatworms.
Nematoda	Roundworms	10,000	Worms pointed at both ends. Include many plant and animal parasites.
Nematomorpha	Horsehair worms	200	Water worms with long, tangled bodies.
Priapulida	Priapulid worms	8	Cucumber-shaped sea worms.
Rotifera	Rotifers	1,600	Microscopic animals with 'wheel-like' head, living in water.
Gastrotricha	Hairy backs	175	Microscopic water animals.
Kinorhyncha	none	100	Microscopic sea animals.
Acantho-cephala	Thorny-headed worms	300	Animal parasites with spiny heads, rather similar to roundworms.
Entoprocta	none	60	Small, polyp-like sea animals.
Ectoprocta	Moss animals or bryozoans	4,000	Small, polyp-like water animals living together in colonies.
Phoronida	Phoronid worms	15	Tube-dwelling sea worms.
Brachiopoda	Lamp shells	260	Small sea animals with clam-like shells but not related to molluscs.
Annelida	Earthworms and relatives	About 7,000	Worms with bodies made up of many similar segments. Bristleworms live in the sea; earthworms live in the soil; leeches have fewer segments and many are blood-suckers.
Sipunculoidea	Peanut worms	250	Plump-bodied sea worms.

Phylum	Common name, if any	No. of species	Description and examples
Echiuroidea	Echiurid worms	60	Sea worms having a few bristles.
Pentastomida	Tongue worms	70	Worm-like animal parasites.
Tardigrada	Water bears	180	Microscopic 8-legged water animals.
Mollusca	Molluscs	More than 46,000	A huge group of animals living in water and on land. Their soft bodies are usually protected by a chalky shell. Include snails, slugs, limpets, tusk shells, mussels, clams, chitons, squids and octopuses.
Chaetognatha	Arrow worms	50	Small, fast-swimming sea animals.
Pogonophora	Beard worms	About 80	Tube-dwelling deep-sea worms. Some recently discovered are 3½ metres long.
Echino-dermata	Starfish and relatives	About 5,500	Slow-moving sea animals whose bodies have a radial (wheel-spokes) plan. They comprise starfish; brittle stars; sea urchins; sea lilies and sea cucumbers.
Hemi-chordata	Acorn worms and relatives	90	Worm-like sea animals which may be remotely related to backboned animals.
Chordata	Chordates	About 1,300, plus all the species of back-boned animals	Animals that all have, at some time in their lives, an internal body-supporting rod called the notochord. They include seasquirts; salps; lancelets and all the backboned animals or vertebrates.

1   2   3   4   5

Univalve shells are either left-handed (1) or right-handed (2).

The chambered nautilus (3) is in the cephalopod group. while the mussel (4) and the mantle scallop (5) shells are bivalves.

47

Arthropods

Arthropods form the biggest single group in the animal kingdom, with somewhere around a million species. The phylum includes insects, crustaceans, arachnids (spiders and their allies), centipedes, millipedes, velvet worms, and horseshoe crabs.

Nearly all arthropods have hard skeletons outside the body. This 'exoskeleton' is jointed like a suit of armour for ease of movement. The name arthropod means 'having jointed legs', and all arthropods do have jointed legs: insects have six and spiders eight, while centipedes and millipedes have a great many more. Crustaceans such as crabs and lobsters have ten walking legs; but other crustaceans have a variable number.

A lacewing performs aerial gyrations. These delicate insects belong to the group called Neuroptera, which also includes the ant lions. In contrast to the inoffensive-looking adult insects, Neuroptera larvae are ferocious in appearance, with relatively huge jaws.

Insects

Above: A potter wasp makes a clay cell stocked with caterpillars, in which she lays her eggs. She seals the pot and flies away to die.

A Golden-ringed dragonfly, one of the fastest flying insects.

Of all forms of life, the most varied are the insects. More than 700,000 different species are known, and more are being classified each year. The number of individual insects is almost beyond calculation.

An adult insect has six legs, and a body in three sections covered with a hard casing known as an exoskeleton. Most insects have wings. Their eyes are made up of up to 30,000 tiny lenses called facets, each facet contributing a tiny part of the whole view to the insect's brain. Insects have senses of smell and taste, and many kinds can hear, too. They have cold blood which may be colourless, green, or yellow.

Insects are grouped into 33 orders, each containing many families, genera, and species.

Apterygote insects are the simplest kind. They have no wings, and the young are similar in appearance to the adults, except in size.

Exopterygote insects mostly have wings, and pass through three stages of development—egg, nymph, and adult. They include dragonflies (order Odonata), crickets (order Orthoptera), earwigs (Dermaptera), and bugs (Hemiptera).

Endopterygote insects are also winged, and go through four stages—egg, larva, pupa, and adult. They include butterflies and moths (Lepidoptera), flies (Diptera), and beetles and weevils (Coleoptera).

MIRACLE OF METAMORPHOSIS
A child is a miniature version of an adult person—but butterflies and moths and other endopterygote insects go through some amazing changes during their life. These changes are called metamorphosis.

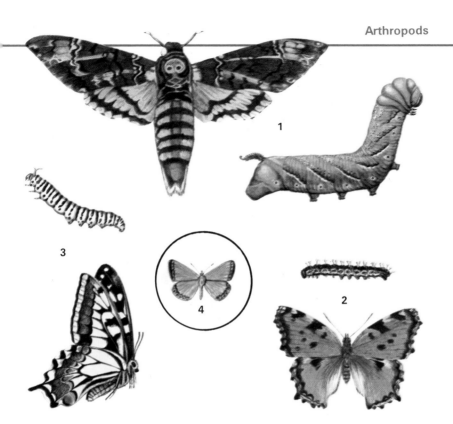

The insect starts as an egg, laid by the female adult. The egg hatches, to produce a larva, an immature insect. Caterpillars form the larval stage of a butterfly or moth lifecycle. The larva eats and grows for some time. Then it makes itself a smooth, hard case for its next stage of life, the pupal stage. As a pupa, the insect undergoes a truly astonishing change. The body is broken down to its basic tissues, and rebuilt into its adult form. The adult insect emerges from the case.

Some insects undergo incomplete metamorphosis, leaving out the pupal stage. For example, the dragonfly (order Odonata) goes from egg to nymph—a wingless form—and then sheds its outer skin and emerges as an adult.

Butterflies, moths and their caterpillars. The death's head moth (1) of Europe and Africa, the large tortoiseshell (2) of Europe, the swallowtail (3) found mainly in the tropics. Circled (4) is the tiny common blue of Europe, North Africa and northern Asia.

Springtail   **Flea**

GRASSHOPPERS

Grasshoppers are leaping insects of the families Acrididae or Tettigoniidae common in fields and along roadsides in most parts of the world. A grasshopper can leap a distance about 20 times the length of its body: if Man were able to do the same, he could jump about 36 yards (33 metres). In certain parts of the world people eat grasshoppers—dried, jellied, or ground into a meal.

Among the most destructive of all insects are locusts (family Acrididae), a kind of grasshopper. Every so often these creatures form huge swarms, flying in dense clouds that almost obscure the light of the Sun. When such a swarm lands it devours every living plant. One swarm in the Red Sea region in 1899 was estimated to cover an area of 2,000 square miles (5,200 sq km).

Right: Grasshoppers sing by rubbing a row of tiny pegs on a hindleg over veins on a forewing.

Below: Food shortages cause the normally solitary locusts to give birth to young that are different in shape and colour from their parents, and which migrate in large and devastating swarms.

Grasshopper

Right: The eye of a Common house-fly. Insects' eyes are made of up to 30,000 hexagonal lenses; they see things as rather blurred patterns of dots.

THE HELPFUL FLY

Flies include many disease-carrying pests, but some flies are useful, especially to scientists. One of the most useful insects for the researcher is the fruit fly or vinegar fly, (genus *Drosophila*). Fruit flies breed fast—a new generation is born about every two weeks—and for this reason they are valuable for the study of heredity and evolution. Any mutations show up quickly, and changes in the fruit flies to correspond with their environment can be studied easily. These insects are attracted to overripe fruit, wine, beer, vinegar—and even fresh paint. They breed prolifically, and one pair of fruit flies will produce thousands of descendants a year.

53

THE DESTRUCTIVE BEETLE

Beetles include the most useful and destructive of insects. They eat a great variety of things and many of them act as natural scavengers, disposing of dead animal and vegetable matter. But they cannot distinguish between wanted and unwanted material, so from Man's point of view they are often a pest.

Ladybirds (family Coccinellidae) eat aphids such as greenfly which damage plants.

Skin beetles (Dermestidae) eat stored food, furs, wool, and other animal substances. Museum beetles (*Anthrenus museorum*) make a speciality of eating museum specimens— though curators use leather beetles (*Dermestes maculatus*) to clean up skeletons for display!

Glowworms and **fireflies** (family Lampyridae) are beetles that emit a phosphorescent glow at night.

Short circuit beetles (*Scobicia declivis*) bore through lead cables, letting in water that causes short circuits.

Below: Members of the beetle family. 1. The ladybird kills harmful insects such as aphids. 2. The longhorned beetle. 3. The great diving beetle which breathes through its tail-tip. 4. The aptly named rhinoceros beetle. 5. The stag beetle— the males have antler-like mandibles (jaws).

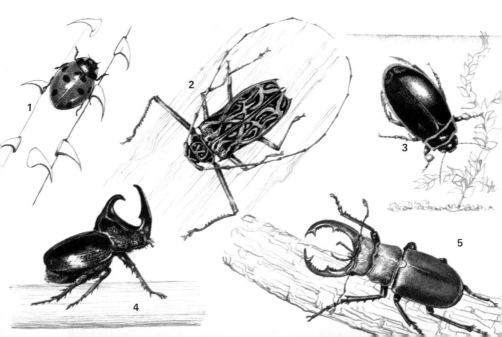

SOCIAL INSECTS

Social insects like bees, wasps, ants, and termites live in rigidly organized communities. Ants are divided into queens, males (who do no work), and the female workers. Large-headed workers called soldiers defend the nest, which has several chambers for different purposes.

Giant nests like this are built by tiny termites.

Weaver ants make a nest by binding leaves with silk.

Wild worker honeybees shape wax for the comb. They manufacture this wax in their bodies and extrude it from pores in their abdomen.

Hard earned honey
Survival often means sheer hard work—and especially so for honeybees. To collect just one ounce (28 g) of honey a bee may have to fly about 80 miles (130 km)!

Right: A bee injecting venom into the body of an enemy. The sting of a honeybee can only be used once, but a bumble bee's may be withdrawn from the enemy and used again.

RECORD INSECTS

Largest group of insects are the beetles (order Coleoptera), of which 300,000 species are known

Most primitive insects are the silverfish (order Thysanura) and their close relatives. They are thought to be the oldest insects known in fossil form.

Largest insects are several forms of beetles (Coleoptera). They include the goliath beetle (genus *Goliathus*) of Central Africa; the rhinoceros beetle (*Dynastes hercules*), and the longhorned beetle (*Titanus giganteus*), which have all been found at sizes between 5 inches and 7 inches (12.5—17.5 cm) long.

Longest insects are varieties of stick insects (genera *Palophus* and *Pharnacia*), known to grow more than 12 inches (30 cm) long.

Smallest insects are feather-winged beetles (family Ptiliidae), which measure less than 1/100 of an inch (0.25 mm) long.

Spiders, etc

Spiders and their various relations belong to the class of arthropods called arachnids. The name comes from the Greek legend of a maiden named Arachne, who challenged the goddess Athena to a weaving contest. When Arachne's tapestry was torn up by the angry goddess she hanged herself—but Athena changed her into a spider and the tapestry into a web.

Arachnids' bodies are divided into two main parts, joined at a sort of waist. All have eight legs. There are four main kinds of arachnids:

Mites and ticks make up the order Acarina. There are at least 10,000 species known.

Spiders form the order Araneae. There are more than 20,000 species.

Scorpions form the order Scorpiones, with 600 species. They have powerful stings which they use to defend themselves and sometimes to stun their prey.

Harvestmen form the order Opiliones, or Phalangida.

In addition there are the tiny pseudo-scorpions, which have no stings, and some other scorpion-like orders.

Dicing with death
The pitcher plant is a carnivorous plant which lures insects into its liquid-filled cup, where they drown. But one spider, *Misumenops nepenthecola,* dices with death—it lives inside the pitcher, just clear of the liquid, eating insects before they fall in and drown.

Many spiders spin delicate silken webs to ensnare their prey. The trap-door spider digs a burrow lined with silk. The hinged door keeps the burrow clean and enables the spider to ambush its prey.

Above: The female wolf spider carries her young on her back, but if one falls off she will not stop. If the spiderling cannot climb back on, it dies.

Above: The water spider breathes air but lives under water! It does this by trapping a store of air bubbles in a bell of silk.

Above: The black widow is the most notorious of the poisonous spiders, but its bite is very rarely fatal to Man.

THE HARVESTMAN

One arachnid is seen most often at harvest time and is called the harvestman for that reason. In North America it is known as daddy longlegs, the name given to the cranefly in Britain. The harvestman looks like a very long-legged spider, but the two parts of its body are joined almost as a unit. It belongs to the order Opiliones, or Phalangida, and there are about 2,400 species. The French call them *faucheurs*, reapers, because they can swing each leg like a mower with a scythe.

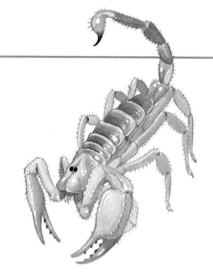

> **The hunters**
> Wolf spiders (family Hycosidae) and jumping spiders (family Salticidae) hunt their prey on the ground. They stalk their victims by sight, and the jumping spiders leap on them and catch them.

The scorpion's powerful venom is in the tip of its tail.

Spiders eat insects in much larger numbers than most people realize. In England and Wales, for example, there are well over 2,000,000 spiders in every acre of meadow land. It has been estimated that in one year the spiders in the country eat a weight of insects that exceeds the total weight of the human population of England and Wales.

SPIDERS AND SCORPIONS

Largest spiders are some of the bird-eating spiders (family Theraphosidae) of South America, whose bodies are more than 3 inches (7.6 cm) long with a leg span of more than 10 inches (25 cm).

Smallest spiders are members of the genus *Microlinypheus,* from Australia, whose body length is less than 1/25 inch (1 mm).

Most notorious of venomous spiders is the black widow (*Latrodectus mactans*), whose bite can kill young children. There are several other equally venomous types.

Largest scorpions are of the genus *Pandinus,* found in Africa; *Pandinus imperator* is known to reach a length of more than 8 inches (20 cm).

Most dangerous scorpions belong to the genus *Centruroides* of North America (species *sculpturatus* and *gertschi*) and *Androctonus australis* of North Africa. Their sting can kill a man in 45 minutes.

Centipedes and Millipedes

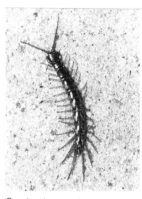

Centipedes paralyse and kill prey with venom from the front pair of legs. Their skin is not waterproof so they live in damp places to stop their body fluids drying up.

Most people probably think that the only difference between centipedes and millipedes is in the number of legs. But in fact the number of legs—of which both have plenty —is the one thing they have in common. Scientists used to group them together in the class Myriapoda (many-footed) but now divide them into two separate classes, Chilopoda (centipedes) and Diplopoda (millipedes).

Centipedes are ferocious little carnivores. They eat insects, earthworms, slugs, and other small creatures, and are cannibals as well. They have a pair of poison claws with which they kill their prey, and they can inflict a painful bite. The body consists of many segments, each of which has one pair of legs. Centipedes vary from about 1 inch (2.5 cm) to 12 inches (30 cm) long, and can have from 14 to 350 legs. There are 2,000 species.

Millipedes are vegetarians, and like to eat decaying material. They range in size from 2/25 inch (2 mm) long to about 12 inches (30 cm). Although the name means 'thousand-footed' even the longest millipede has only about 400 legs, generally two pairs to each segment. The animals walk by contracting their legs in groups, then spreading out in a sort of ripple. Millipedes moult at intervals, adding new sections every time they do so. The main weapons are stink glands. There are 8,000 species.

Left: A millipede and a pill millipede. Many millipedes secrete poison as a defence against enemies. Pill millipedes curl up to protect themselves.

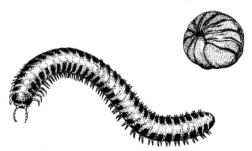

Centipedes are good mothers. They lay clusters of eggs and curl tightly around them to guard them until they hatch. Other centipedes lay one egg at a time and leave it to hatch by itself. Some millipede mothers also guard their young, while others seal the eggs into nests made of earth and saliva.

Centipedes' bodies are made up of 15 to almost 20 jointed segments, each bearing a pair of legs. They are found all over the world.

Onychophora is a class that contains only one type of invertebrate animal, commonly called Peripatus or velvet worm. It forms a link between two great animal groups. It is in many ways like an arthropod, and in many others like an annelid worm.

BY A LEG

Largest centipede is the Giant scolpender (*Scolpendra gigantea*) of Central America. Its body is up to 12 inches (30 cm) long, and 1 inch (2.5 cm) wide, and it is large enough to feed on mice and lizards, as well as insects.

Centipedes with most legs are those in the group Geophilomorpha. Adults may have up to 177 pairs of legs, or 354 legs altogether.

Largest millipedes are several species that are up to about 12 inches (30 cm) in length, and may be as much as $\frac{3}{4}$ inch (2 cm) in diameter.

Millipedes with most legs are generally the oldest. Several species are known to have almost 200 segments, with a total of legs approaching 750.

Crustaceans

Crustaceans, like insects and spiders, belong to the vast group of animals known as arthropods. They are found in nearly all the waters of the world—lakes, ponds, rivers, and oceans. Although some do live on land, they have been nicknamed 'the insects of the sea'.

There are about 45,000 species of crustaceans, and the group contains animals of all shapes and sizes. Well-known crustaceans include barnacles, crabs, lobsters, shrimps, and woodlice. There is also a vast number of smaller, lesser-known species, like fairy shrimps, water fleas, and copepods.

Crustaceans vary in size from the minute water fleas (order Cladocera), some of which are only 0.25 mm long, to the Japanese Spider crab, whose legs may span 10 feet (3 m).

Like other arthropods, crustaceans have segmented bodies. They have outer skeletons —exoskeletons—made of a substance called chitin and strengthened with lime. This covering is soft at the joints to allow movement.

Above: Barnacle larvae swim freely through the sea, but when they become adult they settle down for the rest of their lives. Their perfect home is a shady spot with a rough surface to cling to.

Right: A Ghost crab excavating its burrow.
Below: The blind, colourless woodlouse sheds its skin as soon as it is born and feeds on it.

Crabs and lobsters (order Decapoda) have an unusual method of escaping from enemies: they break off a limb if caught. The break normally occurs on one particular joint, the third from the body. A blood clot forms which prevents bleeding, and a new limb starts growing almost immediately. After a few moults it reaches the same size as the other limbs.

A swimming crab from the Pacific. Most crabs breathe through gills, but the gill cavities of true land crabs are so enlarged they act as lungs.

RECORDS: CRUSTACEANS

Largest crustacean is the Japanese Spider crab (*Machrocheira kaempferi*) with a body length of about 1 foot (30 cm) and a limb span of about 10 feet (3 m).

Smallest crustaceans are some species of water fleas (order Cladocera), which have an overall span of less than 0.25mm.

Largest lobster is the American lobster (*Homarus americanus*), which can measure about 3 feet (1 m) long and weigh up to 40 lb (18 kg).

Invertebrates: Phylum Arthropoda: 'joint-legged animals'

CLASS Insecta: Insects: six-legged arthropods			
Order	Common name, if any	No. of species	Description and examples
Diplura	2-pronged bristletails	400	Small, primitive, wingless insects. Live under stones and leaves.
Thysanura	Silverfish and relatives	350	Primitive wingless insects. Silverfish are common kitchen pests.
Collembola	Springtails	1,100	Tiny, primitive, wingless; spring about on soil and water surfaces.
Protura	none	45	Small, primitive, wingless.
Odonata	Dragonflies, etc	4,500	Two pairs of wings. Very large eyes.
Ephemeroptera	Mayflies	1,300	Two pairs of wings. Spends brief adult life flying over water.
Plecoptera	Stoneflies	1,300	Weak fliers, always seen near water.
Mantodea	Praying mantises	1,800	Typical large 'praying' forelegs.
Phasmida	Stick insects	2,000	Resemble twigs. Also leaf insects.
Orthoptera	Grasshoppers and relatives	10,000	Most have hopping legs. Also includes crickets and locusts.
Blattaria	Cockroaches	3,500	Leathery bodies. Common house pests.
Isoptera	Termites	1,900	Live in colonies. Have several castes.
Notoptera	none	6	Wingless. Live on cold mountains.
Dermaptera	Earwigs	900	Leathery bodies, with pincers.
Embioptera	Web-spinners	150	Tiny, tropical, live under stones.
Zoraptera	none	16	Tiny, tropical, live in rotten wood.
Psocoptera	Book lice	1,000	Tiny, live in books or timber.
Mallophaga	Bird lice	2,600	Infest birds, eat feathers, skin.
Anoplura	Sucking lice	250	Human body louse, etc. Suck blood.
Hemiptera	Bugs	55,000	All have piercing beak to suck up plant juices, blood, or insect juices.
Thysanoptera	Thrips	5,000	Small plant-juice suckers.
Neuroptera	Lacewings and Ant lions	4,000	Delicate, lacy wings. Their larvae have ferocious, poisonous jaws.
Megaloptera	Alderflies	500	Lacy wings. Always seen near water.
Raphidiodea	Snakeflies	80	Wood insects with snake-like head.
Mecoptera	Scorpionflies	300	Male has scorpion-like tail.
Strepsiptera	none	300	Tiny parasites in bees, wasps, ants.
Trichoptera	Caddis flies	3,500	Hairy wings. Aquatic larvae build cases.
Coleoptera	Beetles, weevils, etc	300,000	Most species of any group. Range from microscopic to largest insects.
Zeugloptera	none	100	Tiny, moth-like pollen eaters.
Lepidoptera	Butterflies and moths	120,000	Butterflies are brightly coloured day fliers. Moths mostly nocturnal.
Diptera	True flies	75,000	One pair of wings. Include gnats, midges, mosquitoes, clegs.

Order	Common name, if any	No. of species	Description and examples
Siphonaptera	Fleas	1,800	Wingless blood-suckers of birds and mammals. Good jumpers.
Hymenoptera	Bees, wasps, ants etc	100,000	Four wings. Some (bees etc) live in complex colonies.
CLASS Crustacea: water-dwelling arthropods			
Subclass Cephalocarida	none	4	Tiny, shrimp-like, primitive.
Branchiopoda	Water fleas	1,200	Very tiny. Also, brine shrimps.
Ostracoda	Mussel shrimps	20,000	Very tiny; mussel-like shell.
Copepoda	Copepods	4,500	Very tiny; vast numbers in plankton.
Mystacocarida	none	3	Tiny sand dwellers.
Branchiura	Fish lice	75	Small parasites of fishes.
Cirripedia	Barnacles etc	800	Also includes many parasites.
Malacostraca	Crabs and relatives	18,000	Also lobsters, shrimps, prawns, and the land-dwelling woodlice.
CLASS Pycnogonida	Sea spiders	About 500	Spidery, 'all legs', 6–7 pairs.
CLASS Merostomata	King crabs, or horseshoe crabs	5	*Not* crabs: more closely related to spiders and scorpions.
CLASS Arachnida: eight-legged land arthropods			
Order Araneae	Spiders	20,000	Poison fangs; spin silk thread.
Solifugae	Sun spiders	570	Large, tropical, spider-like.
Acarina	Mites, ticks	10,000	Mostly tiny; many are parasites.
Ricinulei	none	About 15	Very small, live in tropical mould.
Opiliones	Harvestmen	2,400	Also called daddy long legs.
Scorpionida	Scorpions	600	Large pincers; curved stinging tail.
Pseudo-scorpionida	False scorpions	1,100	Small arachnids with pincers but no stings.
Uropygi	Whip scorpions	105	Small, with fangs and whip-like tail.
Palpigradi	Micro-whip scorpions	21	Tiny soil dwellers, with long tail but no sting.
CLASS Pauropoda	none	60	Tiny 10- or 12-legged soil dwellers.
CLASS Diplopoda	Millipedes	8,000	Long bodies with up to 200 legs. Plant feeders living all over world.
CLASS Chilopoda	Centipedes	2,000	Predators with poison fangs, also with long bodies and many legs.
CLASS Symphyla	none	120	Small, obscure dwellers under leaves and stones. Long feelers.
CLASS Onychophora	Velvet worms	About 120	*Peripatus* and other species are links between annelid worms and arthropods.

VERTE- BRATES

The vertebrates—animals with backbones— are the most advanced animals alive. There are seven living classes of vertebrates: lampreys and hagfish, cartilaginous fish, bony fish, amphibians, reptiles, birds, and mammals. All vertebrates have a spinal cord enclosed in the backbone. They have an internal skeleton, and are always bilaterally symmetrical—the left and right sides of their bodies are mirror images. All but the most primitive have a cranium (brain case) and land-dwelling vertebrates generally have two pairs of limbs. Some, such as the snakes, have lost their limbs during evolution. Vertebrates can grow much larger than invertebrates, because the internal skeleton gives the animal support while it is growing. The first vertebrates, small fish-like creatures without jaws or paired fins, appeared about 480 million years ago.

Bony fishes are the most specialised and varied vertebrates living in water. The colourful firemouth cichlid is a tropical bony fish popular in aquaria.

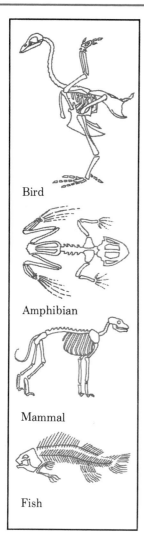

Bird

Amphibian

Mammal

Fish

The powerful sucker of a sea lamprey. The jawless lamprey punctures the skin of other fish, using the teeth lining its tongue, and sucks in the victim's blood.

The bone structures of all vertebrates are basically similar; all are bilaterally symmetrical (the left and right sides are alike) and land vertebrates usually have four limbs. The spinal column is protected by a chain of little bones called vertebrae.

Fishes

JAWLESS FISH

Hagfish and lampreys are the most primitive of fish. Instead of jaws they have a circular mouth with rasping teeth.

Hagfish feed mainly on worms and dead fish, but also attack fish hooked by fishermen. The hagfish covers its prey with slime from glands on its body, and bores into it with its rasping mouth.

Some lampreys also attack fish in this way, but feed mainly on their victim's blood. Their glands secrete a substance which prevents it from clotting. Other lampreys suck in worms and other small aquatic animals.

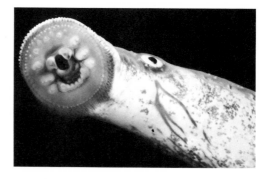

Left: The blue-spotted reef ray is one of the cartilaginous fish, with a skeleton made of gristle, not bone. Its mouth and gills are on its underside.

THE GRISTLY SHARK

Sharks, skates, rays, and chimeras belong to the class of fish called Chondrichthyes, the cartilaginous fishes. Their skeletons are made of cartilage or gristle rather than bone.

This group contains some very dangerous and ferocious fish. Sharks are beautiful, streamlined animals, but danger lies in their well-developed jaws and in the sharp, tooth-like scales that cover their skin.

There are about 200 species of shark. The largest is the Whale shark, which can reach 60 feet (18 m) but which feeds harmlessly on plankton. The most deadly is probably the White shark (*Carcharodon carcharias*). Found in tropical seas, it is a notorious man-eater greatly feared by swimmers.

SHARKS AND RAYS

Largest shark is the Whale shark (*Rhincodon typus*) which can reach a length of between 50 and 60 feet (15—18 m) and weigh several tonnes.

Largest rays are the devil rays (family Mobulidae) which measure up to 20 feet (6 m) across, and 'fly' through the water by flapping their pectoral fins like wings. Some can even leap quite high into the air.

BONY FISH

The largest group of vertebrates is the fish. There are about 13,000 species, most of which have bony skeletons. The bony fish (Osteichthyes) include all the familiar fish like eels, herring, minnows, and salmon as well as a large and bewildering variety of little-known species.

There are two main groups of bony fishes. The first, the Crossopterygii, have fleshy fins. This group includes the ancient coelacanth.

The second, and by far the larger group, is the ray-finned fishes (sub-class Actinopterygii), which includes all the other bony fish. This group ranges from the primitive sturgeon, one of the largest bony fishes, to the smallest of all fish, the tiny gobies of the Philippines.

The flying fish can glide for over half a minute.

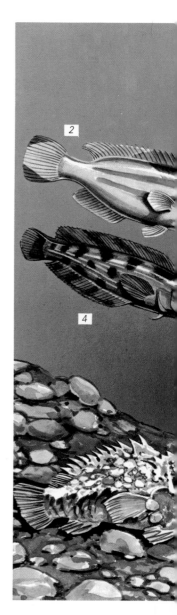

Fish travel considerable distances in search of food. The remora (*Remora remora*) travels with the minimum of effort. Its first dorsal fin has evolved into a large oval sucker, with raised edges and a ridged surface, with which it attaches itself to larger fish like sharks. The sucker can only be dislodged if the remora voluntarily swims forwards. The remora shares its host's food and also eats smaller fishes. If the host dies or is caught, the remora drops off. In some parts of the world remoras are used as living harpoons for catching turtles. Attached to a line, they are allowed to swim out and fix themselves to turtles, then gently pulled back to the hunters' boats.

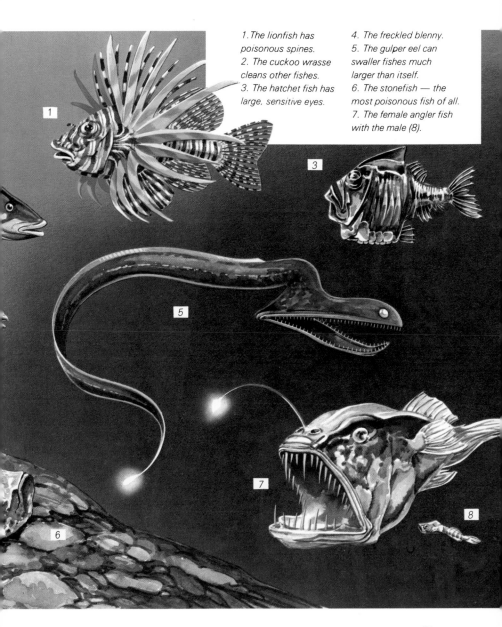

1. The lionfish has poisonous spines.
2. The cuckoo wrasse cleans other fishes.
3. The hatchet fish has large, sensitive eyes.
4. The freckled blenny.
5. The gulper eel can swaller fishes much larger than itself.
6. The stonefish — the most poisonous fish of all.
7. The female angler fish with the male (8).

NESTING FISH

Most bony fish reproduce rather haphazardly. Eggs are left unprotected and thousands die or are eaten. Sticklebacks are more careful – they build nests.

The Three-spined stickleback (*Gasterosteus aculeatus*) is found in ponds and streams throughout Europe. At breeding time the male builds a fine, tubular nest from roots, stems, and leaves, cemented with a sticky fluid or mucus from his kidneys. He then finds a female and chases her into the nest, where she lays a few eggs before being chased out again! The male repeats this process with several different females until his nest is full of eggs. He then guards it, chasing away all other fish, including former mates. In three weeks, the young have hatched, and the male takes the nest apart. He continues to look after the young for another two weeks until they can fend for themselves.

The stickleback is one of the few fishes to build a nest for its eggs.

Among sea horses, it is the male which carries and hatches the eggs in a special breeding pouch.

FLATFISH

Flatfishes such as halibut, plaice, and sole (order Pleuronectiformes) are not born flat. Unlike the cartilaginous rays and skates, they lie on their sides, not on their bellies. The young start life with a normal cylinder shape, but after a few days one eye begins to move from one side to the other. The fish ends up with two eyes on one side of its head. As this happens, the fish's body becomes flattened. It moves down to the sea-bed and settles with its eye-side uppermost. All flatfishes are well camouflaged to match the sea-bed, and can change colour to some extent. No flatfish live in fresh water.

Above: Fish are still an important source of food.

Right: Commercially, plaice are the most important flatfish. These prolific breeders have twisted mouths, with the lower side more developed and armed with teeth.

Left: The mirror carp and, below it, the leather carp. The former has two rows of large scales, while the latter is scaleless.

Goldfish (*Carassius auratus*) are among the few fish that may be described as domesticated. The goldfish is a species of carp (family Cyprinidae), and has been bred in captivity for more than 1000 years. The original goldfish was a plain-coloured carp which the Chinese began to keep in aquariums and breed for its potential colours in the 10th century AD.

A Whale shark—the largest of all fish. The smallest fish (inset) is the Dwarf goby which grows to ½ inch (1.25 cm) at most.

Fish, like all other animals, need oxygen to survive. They get it from the water in which they live. Water is taken in through the mouth and passed through gills. These contain blood vessels, which filter out the oxygen dissolved in the water. The oxygen is taken into the bloodstream, and the water expelled through vertical openings behind the fish's head.

Normally, when a pond or stream dries up in hot weather or water becomes stagnant and is lacking in oxygen, the fish inhabitants die. But there are some species that can survive in such conditions. They are 'lungfishes'—possibly the last survivors of the fishes that developed into land creatures many millions of years ago.

The mudskipper is a successful 'fish out of water'. It crawls round the mud of tropical swamps at low tide. It can breathe air as well as water, but it needs constantly to renew the supply of water to its gill chambers by returning to pools left by the tide.

FISH RECORDS

The longest bony fish is the beluga (*Huso huso*), a kind of sturgeon found in the USSR. It has been known to grow up to 23 feet 7 inches (7.2 m) in length, and reach a weight of 3000 lb (1360 kg).

The heaviest bony fish is the Ocean sunfish (*Mola mola*) which can weigh up to 2 tonnes.

The smallest fish and also the smallest vertebrate is the Dwarf goby, found in fresh water in the Philippines and the Marshall Islands. The maximum size for these tiny fish is half an inch (1.25 cm).

CLASS Agnatha: jawless fishes			
Order	Common name	No. species	Description and examples
Cyclostomata	Lampreys and hagfishes	45	Parasites and scavengers with rasping, jawless mouths.

CLASS Chondrichthyes: fishes with a cartilage skeleton			
Order	Common name	No. species	Description and examples
Selachii	Sharks	200	Streamlined bodies. Range from small dogfishes to giant whale shark.
Batoidea	Rays and skates	350	Flattened bodies. Include giant manta rays and sawfishes.
Chimeriformes	Chimeras	25	Strange-looking deep-sea fishes which grind up shellfish for food.

CLASS Osteichthyes: fishes with a bony skeleton			
Order	Common name	No. species	Description and examples
Polypteriformes	Bichirs	12	Archaic bony fishes with air-breathing lungs, in African rivers.
Acipenseriformes	Sturgeons	22	Archaic river mudgrubbers. Include giants that produce caviar (roe).
Amiiformes	Bowfin	1	Archaic predatory fish of North American rivers.
Semionotiformes	Garpikes	7	Archaic pike-like fishes of North American rivers, up to 3 metres long.
Crossopterygii	Coelacanth	1	A lobefin fish—the last survivor of the fishy ancestors of land animals.
Dipnoi	Lungfishes	5	Lobefin fishes with lungs—another very ancient group.
Elopiformes	Tarpons	12	Large, rather primitive teleost fishes (all the following are teleosts).
Anguilliformes	Eels	300	Long-bodied fishes mostly of the sea.
Notacanthiformes	Spiny eels	20	Deep-sea fishes resembling eels.
Clupeiformes	Herring and relatives	350	Sea fishes also including sprat, anchovy, pilchard, sardine.
Osteoglossiformes	Bony tongues	16	Rather primitive river fishes. *Arapaima* is up to 5 metres long.
Mormyriformes	Mormyrids	150	'Elephant snout fish' etc. African.
Salmoniformes	Salmon, trout	500	Also includes pike, deep-sea fishes.
Myctophiformes	Lantern fish	300	Luminous deep-sea fishes.
Ctenothrissiformes	Macristid fish	1	Deep-sea fish related to lantern fishes.

Order	Common name	No. species	Description and examples
Gonorhynch-iformes	Milk fish	15	Fishes related to both carp and lantern fishes.
Cypriniformes	Carp and relatives	350	River fishes also including goldfish, bream, minnows, roach, electric eel etc.
Siluriformes	Catfishes	200	Whiskery barbels on snout. Range from tiny to 3 metres long.
Percopsiformes	Pirate perch	10	Small N. American river fishes.
Batrachoid-iformes	Toadfishes	10	Seabed fishes with poison spines.
Gobiesoc-iformes	Clingfishes	100	Coastal fishes with clinging sucker formed from front fins.
Lophiiformes	Angler fishes	150	Grotesque deep-sea and bottom-dwellers with long 'fishing line'.
Gadiformes	Cod and relatives	450	Also includes haddock, ling, hake, pollack, whiting, coalfish, rockling.
Beryciformes	Whalefishes, squirrelfishes	150	Spiny sea fishes.
Atherin-iformes	Flying fishes, Killifishes	600	Sea surface skimmers with large wing-like fins.
Zeiformes	John Dory etc	60	John Dory has protrusible jaws.
Lampridiformes	Ribbonfish etc	50	Deep-sea, scaleless fishes.
Gasteroste-iformes	Seahorses and relatives	150	Small, with bony armour. Also includes pipefish and sticklebacks.
Channiformes	Snakeheads	5	Lake fishes, can live out of water.
Synbranch-iformes	Swamp eels and cuchias	7	Estuarine fishes which can live out of water for long periods.
Scorpaen-iformes	Gurnards and relatives	700	Spiny fishes also including scorpion-fishes, bullheads etc.
Dactylopter-iformes	Flying gurnards	6	Like gurnards but with wing-like pectoral fins.
Pegasiformes	Sea moths, dragonfishes	4	Heavily armoured tropical fishes with wing-like pectoral fins.
Tetraodont-iformes	Triggerfishes, puffer fishes	250	Coral reef fishes. Puffers blow themselves into spiny ball.
Pleuronect-iformes	Flatfishes	500	Turbot, plaice, dab, sole, flounder, halibut. All bottom-dwellers with both eyes on uppermost side of body.
Perciformes	Perch and relatives, e.g. mackerel, tuna, sea bass	6,500	By far the largest order of fishes, with representatives in rivers, lakes and oceans. Range in size from a centi-metre to several metres (e.g. tuna).

Amphibians

Amphibians—animals that can live both in water and in air—are the last survivors of the first true land vertebrates that ever existed. The first amphibians probably lived about 350 million years ago, at the end of the Devonian period of prehistory. They were not quite the first vertebrates to struggle on to dry land, that honour being reserved for the lobe-finned fishes. The earliest amphibians evolved from these fishes.

In prehistoric times there were eleven orders of amphibians, and many genera and species. Today there are only three orders left, with a total of about 3000 species.

Caecilians (order Apoda or Gymnophiona) are simple worm-like creatures, and the strangest of all amphibians. They live only in tropical regions, and have no limbs.

Newts and salamanders (order Urodela) have limbs and tails in their adult forms. There are eight families of these creatures, and about 50 genera.

Frogs and toads (order Anura) are the best known of all amphibians. They have legs, but the adult forms have no tails. They are divided into about 12 families and 250 genera.

Most amphibians lay their eggs in water. The eggs hatch into a larval form called a tadpole. This immature form eventually turns into the adult by the process of metamorphosis, though this is not so dramatic a change as takes place in the insect world. There is no pupa, and the animal remains active through the metamorphosis. A few amphibians fail to change, a phenomenon known as neoteny — and some actually breed in the immature state.

Left: The fire salamander owes its name to the myth that it could live through fire.

Above: A caecilian—a legless amphibian that looks much like an earthworm. Below: The axolotl, long thought to be a distinct species, is in fact the larva of a salamander that never fully develops because of a hormone deficiency. Nevertheless the axolotl is able to breed.

Left: A frog's powerful hind legs thrust it into the air. The legs of this species — the edible frog — have been eaten as a delicacy since the days of the Romans.

One kind of frog—the clawed frog of Africa—has claws on its back feet. It spends a lot of time in the water, and uses these claws to defend itself. Unlike most frogs, the clawed frog catches its prey with its hands.

FROGS THAT CLIMB TREES

More than 800 species of frogs are not content to live on land but spend most of their lives climbing trees. Tree frogs belong to the family Hylidae. They are specially adapted for their adventurous life, with sticky pads on their feet that enable them to grip twigs and branches. Indeed, a tree frog can even cling to a vertical pane of glass. These animals leap from branch to branch in search of the insects on which they feed, and can land and gobble up their prey in one swift movement. Tree frogs can change colour to match their surroundings.

AMPHIBIAN RECORDS

Largest amphibians are the Giant salamanders (genus *Megalobatrachus*) of China and Japan, specimens of which have been known to grow up to 5 feet (1.5m) long.

Longest-lived amphibians are probably Japanese Giant salamanders (*Megalobatrachus japonicus*), specimens of which have lived up to 60 years in captivity.

Largest frog is the goliath frog (*Gigantorana goliath*) of Africa. This amphibian habitually grows to a body length of 12 inches (30 cm), but many specimens have been reported considerably larger.

Class Amphibia: vertebrates which spend their lives between land and water. Most have tadpole-like young

Order Anura: Frogs and toads

Family	Common name	No. species	Description and examples
Ascaphidae	Hochstetter's frog etc	4	Primitive frogs of New Zealand and North America.
Pipidae	Clawed toads	15	*Xenopus* and Surinam toads, live entirely in water.
Discoglossidae	Midwife toad	10	Male carries frogspawn until hatching.
Rhynophryn-idae	Mexican burrowing toad	1	Lives on Central American coast.
Pelobatidae	none	54	Small, widespread toads.
Bufonidae	Toads	300	Common toad and relatives, live everywhere except Australia.
Ranidae	Frogs	More than 300	Common frog and relatives. Good jumpers which live worldwide.
Hylidae	Tree frogs	600	Widespread: live in trees.
Leptodactyl-idae	none	650	Widespread but little known. Include burrowing frogs of desert country.
Atelopodidae	Arrow-poison frogs etc	About 90	Brilliantly coloured, mainly South American frogs, some with highly poisonous skins.
Rhacophoridae	none	Over 200	Tree-living, frogs of tropics.
Microhylidae	none	Over 200	Tropical. Some hatch out directly as frogs.

Order Urodela: newts and salamanders

Family	Common name	No. species	Description and examples
Hynobiidae	Asiatic land salamanders	30	Primitive. Live mostly on land.
Cryptobranch-idae	Giant salamanders	3	Japanese species up to $1\frac{1}{2}$ metres long. Others in USA and China.
Ambystomidae	Axolotl etc	32	All from N. and Central America. Axolotl is 'grown-up tadpole'.
Salamandridae	Newts, etc	42	Includes many small salamanders.
Amphiumidae	Lamper eels	3	In USA swamps. Almost legless.
Plethodont-idae	Lungless salamanders	183	Breathe through skin only. Aquatic.
Proteidae	Mud puppy etc	6	Permanent tadpoles, with gills.
Sirenidae	Sirens	3	Permanent tadpoles. No hind legs.

Order Apoda: Limbless, wormlike amphibians

Family	Common name	No. species	Description and examples
Cecilidae	Cecilians or apodans	About 170	Burrow through moist soil in hot countries. Some brilliantly coloured.

Reptiles

Reptiles are animals with backbones that live by breathing air. They have cold blood, and in evolution they come after the amphibians and before the mammals. The 5,000 species alive today are all that remain of a group of animals that once dominated the Earth—dinosaurs and other giant forms that died out more than 65 million years ago.

Reptiles vary in size from 2 inches (5 cm) long to 30 feet (9 m) or more. They all have scaly skins, and most of them lay eggs. A few give birth to live young. They have lungs, like mammals, and most reptiles are carnivores.

There are four living orders of Reptiles:

Alligators and **crocodiles**, which form the order Crocodilia, are large, heavily armoured animals that spend most of their time in water. Other members of the order are gavials and caimans.

Tuataras are the only survivors of the order Rhynchocephalia. In prehistoric times there were many members of this order, but now there is only one species, *Sphenodon punctatus*. Tuataras live only on a few offshore islands of New Zealand.

Tortoises, terrapins, and **turtles** make up the order Chelonia. They too are heavily armoured, with only the head and limbs protruding from a hard shell. The shell is in two parts, an upper plate called a carapace, and a lower one called a plastron.

Lizards and **snakes** form the order Squamata. Lizards include chameleons, geckos, iguanas, monitors, and slow-worms.

To anyone but an expert, the tuatara resembles a rather large lizard. In fact, it comes of a much more ancient stock, and is a good example of a living fossil.

Alligators make nests in which to lay their eggs. The female constructs the nest by scraping soil and other debris together, using her tail and sides to push the material about, and sometimes scraping with a hind foot. The nest is usually about 3 ft (1 m) high, and 7 feet (2 m) across. She then digs a cavity in the top of the pile, and lays her eggs in it.

Below: The gavial is a member of the crocodile family. It lives in rivers in India, Malaya, and Sumatra. A fish-eater, it has beak-like jaws which it can move easily from side to side under water.

CROCODILIANS

Crocodilians are large, predatory animals. They have flattish skulls with long snouts, and good teeth. The hind legs are longer than the fore legs. They have a long, stout tail, which is flat in section towards the end. Their armour is formed by bony plates embedded in the animal's skin. The crocodilian heart has four chambers like those of mammals—and unlike those of other reptiles. But like most other reptiles crocodilians lay eggs. Crocodilians are divided into three families.

Gavials or **gharials** form the family Gavialidae. There is only one species, *Gavialis gangeticus,* which lives in various rivers in India, Malaysia and Indonesia. It has a long slender snout, and lives almost entirely on fish.

Crocodiles form the family Crocodylidae. There are 16 species living in tropical parts of Africa, Asia, and America. Most of them live in rivers, but the Estuarine or Salt-water crocodile (*Crocodylus porosus*) is found at sea off coasts of southern Asia and northern Australia. Alligators and caimans are very similar to crocodiles, and live mostly in America or in the Yangtse River in China.

Crocodiles float just under the surface of the water with only their eyes and nostrils showing above. They swallow stones, often carrying several pounds in their stomachs. The stones act as ballast, stabilizing the crocodiles.

Despite their fierce reputation, alligators are in more danger from Man than men are from alligators. High prices offered for their skins to make handbags and other goods mean that hunters will defy conservation laws. A craze for baby alligators as pets means that many are taken from the wild, to die before they reach maturity. American alligators are threatened by land drainage schemes.

Below: The tuatara lives only on some small islands in the Cook Strait, between the North and South Islands of New Zealand. The sole survivor of a group of reptiles common in the Mesozoic age, it grows to about 2 feet (61 cm) long. It lives in burrows made by petrels, one of which is nesting on the left.

A gecko's foot, showing the ridges it uses to cling to smooth surfaces.

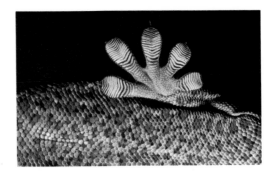

LIZARDS

Lizards and snakes are closely related. Together they form the order Squamata. One obvious difference between these two reptiles is that snakes have no limbs, while nearly all lizards possess legs. Snakes have no eyelids, while almost all lizards have them; and snakes unlike lizards have jaws only loosely connected by ligaments. There are 2,800 species of lizards, in 20 families.

Geckos (family Gekkonidae) are 14 inches (36 cm) or less in length, with flat bodies. They have soft backs, often very rough, and semi-plated underparts. They are nocturnal insect-eaters. Many have pads on their toes which have tiny hooked hairs on them that help the gecko to climb up walls or even run upside down across ceilings.

Agamids (family Agamidae) have scaly skins that are often spiny. They live in rocky areas, and some are tree dwellers. They include the Australian frilled lizard (*Chlamydosaurus kingi*) and the flying dragons (genus *Draco*) of south-eastern Asia.

Iguanas (family Iguanidae) are similar to agamids, but live in the Americas, while agamids are found in Asia, Africa, Australia, and southern Europe.

Typical lizards (family Lacertidae) are the ordinary lizards of Africa, Asia, and Europe, consisting of 150 species. Their American counterparts are the tegus (family Teiidae).

A new tail
Lizards are among animals that have the power of regeneration—that is, growing a new part when the original is lost. The regeneration is confined to the tail. Several kinds of lizards can shed their tails if they are seized by an enemy. The glass snake uses its detachable tail as a means of defence. When attacked in this way, the lizard sheds its tail and glides away to safety. But the tail continues to wriggle encouraging the enemy to continue attacking it and allowing the lizard to get right away.

Monitors are the largest lizards. Some species grow to over 10 feet (3 m) long. They live in Africa, southern Asia and Australia.

Right: A frilled lizard putting on its threatening display. Even larger animals are often deterred by this show.

Gila monsters and **beaded lizards** (family Helodermatidae) live in North American deserts and are the only lizards that have a venomous bite.

Other kinds of lizards include **monitors** (family Varanidae), **chameleons** (Chamaeleontidae), **skinks** (Scincidae), and **slow-worms** (Anguidae).

THE TURTLE FAMILY

Turtles, tortoises, and terrapins form the order of chelonians—but zoologists do not agree which name belongs to which kind of animal. Americans call them all turtles, but sometimes call land-living species tortoises. British zoologists call the land animals tortoises, the marine ones turtles, and those which divide their time between the land and fresh water, terrapins. All chelonians lay eggs that have hard shells covering them. Some eat meat and some are vegetarians. In cold-weather lands they tend to hibernate.

Although they spend most of their time at sea, marine turtles come to land to lay their eggs. The female goes ashore at night on a remote sandy beach and scratches a hole in the sand. There she lays her eggs, in a clutch of up to 200 which may take her several nights to complete. Her task done, she abandons the eggs and returns to sea. The eggs are incubated in the warm sand, and hatch with no aid or further interest from their mother.

The green turtle is one of five species of marine turtles, all of which are large reptiles and one of which, the leathery turtle, is the biggest of the whole turtle-tortoise group.

LIFE ON THE LAND

Tortoises make up the family Testudinidae. They live mostly in the warmer parts of the world, though many are kept as pets in cooler climates. They move slowly on their club-shaped legs, browsing on plants and flowers. Some have dull-coloured shells, but the Madagascan rayed tortoise (*Testudo radiata*) has bright yellow spots and lines on its shell. The tent tortoise (*Testudo tentoria*) has a remarkable shell that looks like a group of little tents.

The Giant tortoises are the biggest of all the chelonians. *Testudo elephantopus* lives only on the Galápagos Islands of the Pacific Ocean, but *Testudo gigantea* is found on several islands of the Indian Ocean, where it is strictly protected. Giant tortoises live to great ages, and specimens have been known to live between 100 and 150 years.

The freshwater tortoises, or terrapins, spend their lives on the banks of rivers and ponds, going into the water to mate and to hunt for fish and amphibians. Some, like the diamond-back terrapin (*Malaclemys terrapin*), spend much time in the water; American box turtles (*Terrapene carolina*) seldom go in.

Below: A Giant tortoise from the Galapagos Islands of the Pacific Ocean. These lumbering giants, once numerous, are now rare. They were easy prey for 19th-century sailors.

Left: A cobra rears and expands its spectacled hood. Cobras are made to 'dance' in this position by snake charmers. Since snakes are deaf, the cobra does not hear the snake charmer's flute, but probably responds to the sounds felt as vibrations — to which snakes are very sensitive.

SNAKES

What makes a snake (suborder Ophidia or Serpentes) different from other reptiles is not just the lack of legs — some lizards have no limbs. It is the way the jaw is hinged. The jaw bones are loosely connected by ligaments, so that they can move apart when the snake swallows its food. In this way a snake can swallow an animal that is two or three times as large as its own head. It has to swallow its food whole because its teeth are not suited to chewing, only to helping the snake swallow its food.

There are about 1800 species of snakes, grouped in 11 families. Only about 300 of them are dangerous to Man. These are the venomous snakes. The venom is not carried in the quick darting tongue, which the snake uses as a sensing organ, but in some of the teeth, which are hollow and are known as poison fangs. The venom of many poisonous snakes is too weak to kill a man, while others are not aggressive and so do little harm anyway. Even so some 30,000 people a year die from snake-bite.

Above: The tracks of a sidewinder. Sidewinding enables a snake to travel fast on loose sand or smooth surfaces. Only a small part of its body touches the ground at any one time. It slithers along the first track, then rears into a loop to start along the next parallel track.

SNAKE NOTES

Skin is changed several times a year by a process known as moulting. The snake slips out of its old skin, leaving it lying like a dummy.

Breathing for most snakes is done on one lung only! The left lung is either missing or greatly reduced in size.

Pit vipers have sense organs that can detect heat—they help in locating prey.

Gastric juices in a snake will digest bones and teeth—but not hair and fur.

Burrowing snakes (several families) burrow into the ground. They feed largely on ants and termites. There are also burrowing cobras.

Most snakes lay eggs which they leave to hatch unattended. The baby snakes fend for themselves from the moment they hatch. A few snakes, including some sea-snakes, give birth to living young.

SNAKE RECORDS

Largest snakes are the anaconda (*Eunectes murinus*) and the reticulated python (*Python reticulatus*), both of which are reported to grow up to 30 feet (9 m) long.

Largest meal eaten by a snake is probably a 200-lb (91-kg) bear, swallowed by a reticulated python.

Largest poisonous snake is the hamadryad or king cobra (*Naja hannah*) of India. Specimens have been known more than 16 feet (5 m) long. It is probably the most dangerous snake, although its venom is not the most toxic.

The anaconda reaches a length of 30 feet (9 m). It waits for its prey by the water's edge and kills them by dragging them underwater.

91

This python has recently eaten a bush pig; the bulge it has made in the snake looks much bigger than the snake's head, but it can disconnect its jaw to eat huge prey.

The largest of all snakes, the boas, anacondas and pythons, are not venomous. They kill their prey by hugging it to death! They are mostly large, some of them reaching 30 feet (9 m), though the famous boa constrictor (*Constrictor constrictor*) averages only about 10 feet (3 m).

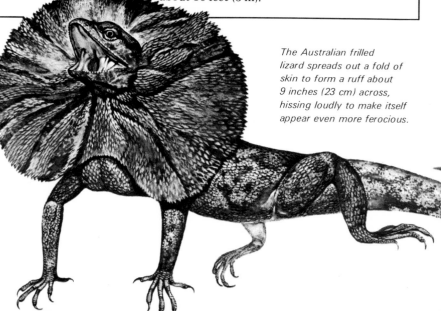

The Australian frilled lizard spreads out a fold of skin to form a ruff about 9 inches (23 cm) across, hissing loudly to make itself appear even more ferocious.

Left: A chameleon — one of the reptiles which changes its colour to match its background. The chameleon can move each of its eyes independently and look in different directions at the same time.

GREEN FOR VICTORY

Many lizards have the ability to change colour—the chameleon is famous for this. But probably the most startling colour variation is provided by the Green anole (*Anolis carolinensis*), a small variety of the iguana. When rival males fight, they are a greyish colour, but when the battle ends the victor turns a bright, triumphant green. The loser? He is yellow!

RECORD REPTILES

Largest reptile is the Estuarine crocodile *(Crocodylus porosus),* which can grow up to 20 feet (6 m) long.

Largest marine turtle is the Leathery or Leatherback turtle (*Dermochelys coriacea*), whose shell may be 6 feet (1.8 m) long, with a flipper-to-flipper stretch of 12 feet (3.6 m), and a weight of more than 1,600 lb (725 kg).

Largest land tortoise is the Giant tortoise (*Testudo gigantea*), which may have a shell 6 feet (1.8 m) long, and a weight of 500 lb (225 kg) or more.

Largest lizard is the Komodo dragon (*Varanus komodoensis*), a monitor which can grow up to 10 feet (3 m) long and weigh 250 lb (113 kg).

Class Reptilia: cold-blooded land vertebrates that lay thick-shelled eggs

Order Chelonia: turtles and tortoises

Family	Common name	No. species	Description and examples
Testudinidae	Tortoises, terrapins	115	All the more well-known tortoises and aquarium terrapins.
Chelydridae	Snappers etc	23	Pond turtles of N. America.
Dermatemydidae	(see right)	1	The Central American river turtle.
Cheloniidae	Marine turtles	5	Green turtle and relatives.
Dermochelyidae	Leathery turtle	1	Largest turtle, weighing up to 550 kg, living in warm seas.
Trionychidae	Soft-shells	22	Widespread river and lake turtles.
Carettochelidae	(see right)	1	The New Guinea pitted-shelled turtle.
Pelomedusidae	Side-necks	14	Withdraw their heads sideways into their shells.
Chelidae	Snake-necks	31	Also bend their long necks sideways.

Order Crocodilia: crocodiles, alligators and gavial

Family	Common name	No. species	Description and examples
Crocodylidae	Crocodiles and alligators	20	These differ in the number and arrangement of their teeth. Rivers and sea.
Gavialidae	Gavial	1	Also called gharial. Very narrow snout.

Order Rhynchocephalia: an ancient group of reptiles with one survivor

Family	Common name	No. species	Description and examples
Sphenodontidae	Tuatara	1	Superficially like a lizard, but its group is older than the dinosaurs.

Order Squamata: lizards and snakes

Family	Common name	No. species	Description and examples
Lacertidae	Lizards	150	The smaller, agile Old World lizards.
Teiidae	Tegus	200	New World equivalents of the above.
Gekkonidae	Geckos	400	Wall-clinging, yapping, tropical.
Chameleontidae	Chameleons	85	Peculiar-looking tree lizards, catching insects with long, sticky tongue.
Iguanidae	Iguanas	700	Large crested lizards; smaller *anoles*.
Agamidae	Agamids	300	Old World versions of iguanas.
Pygopodidae	Flap-footed lizards	13	Australian lizards in which limbs are reduced to two hind flaps.
Scincidae	Skinks	700	Legs may be normal, short or absent.
Feyliniidae	Limbless skinks	4	Snake-like termite eaters.
Dibamidae	(see right)	4	Burrowing lizards. Blind and legless.

Family	Common name	No. species	Description and examples
Anguidae	Slow worms	40	Legs reduced or absent. Forked tongue.
Anniellidae	(see right)	2	Californian legless lizards.
Amphisbenidae	Worm lizards	120	Burrowing, legless lizards. Thick tails.
Xantusiidae	Night lizards	11	Nocturnal and big-eyed like geckos.
Gerrosauridae	Plated lizards	25	African desert lizards.
Cordylidae	Girdle-tailed lizards	23	African grassland and scrub lizards.
Xenosauridae	(see right)	4	Crocodile lizards and relatives.
Helodermat-idae	Poison lizards	2	Gila monster and beaded lizard.
Lanthanotidae	(see right)	1	The earless monitor, a largish lizard.
Varanidae	Monitors	24	Largest of lizards: up to 4 metres long.
Boidae	Constricting snakes	70	Largest snakes: non-poisonous, with vestiges of hind limbs. Boa; anaconda, python.
Typhlopidae	Blind snakes	150	Burrowers, with head shield.
Anomalepidae	none	20	S. American blind burrowers. Head shield.
Leptotyphlop-idae	Thread snakes	40	Blind burrowers of Africa and America.
Uropeltidae	(see right)	43	Indian shield-tailed snakes. Burrowers.
Aniliidae	Pipe snakes	10	S. American burrowers. Hind limb vestiges.
Xenopeltidae	(see right)	1	The sunbeam snake of Asia. Burrower.
Acrochordidae	(see right)	2	Asian sea snakes.
Colubridae	Colubrids	1,100	Widespread. Some venomous, e.g. boomslang.
Elapidae	Cobra family	200	All highly venomous. Mambas, sea snakes, coral snakes, king cobra etc.
Viperidae	Vipers	100	All highly venomous. Adder, puff adder, rattlesnakes, gaboon viper, etc.

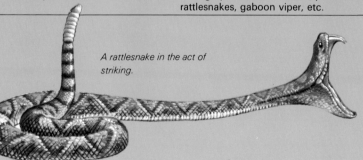

A rattlesnake in the act of striking.

Birds

Birds are animals with feathers, wings, and beaks. Nearly all of them can fly. They are directly descended from reptiles, and many of them have one obvious link with their ancestors—scales on their legs. The link between reptiles and birds is provided by two prehistoric creatures, *Archaeopteryx* and *Archaeornis*, which lived at the time of the dinosaurs. They had feathers and could fly, but also had many reptilian features including teeth, a long bony tail and wing claws.

There are nearly 11,000 species of birds, and they are grouped into 27 orders. Birds can be classified in many different ways. Waterbirds spend their lives on or near water; they include wildfowl—swans, geese, and ducks—and all the various gulls. Perching birds are land-based birds that spend their lives in trees or other high places when not flying. Birds of prey hunt small animals.

One of the most widespread of European passerine or perching birds, the chaffinch.

A scarlet cock-of-the-rock, found in the tropical forests of South America. Its bill is concealed by its curious helmet-like crest.

BIRDS OF PREY

Birds of prey are the hunters of the skies. They include eagles, falcons, buzzards, hawks, owls, and vultures. Birds of prey have keen eyesight, and probably also a good sense of smell. Their feet have curved talons for grasping prey. Some, such as the kestrel (family Falconidae), can hover over one spot, while they scan the ground for likely victims. Owls hunt at night for small mammals and birds. Falcons are among the fastest of all fliers. The biggest birds of prey are eagles, which can carry off young lambs and other animals up to about 20 lb (9 kg). Vultures and kites live on carrion.

PERCHING BIRDS

Perching birds can go to sleep while sitting on a branch—and the more deeply they sleep, the less likely they are to fall. As the bird relaxes its leg joints bend more. The grip of its claws is controlled by long tendons running round the outside of these joints; as the joints bend the tendons are stretched, tightening the hold of the claws.

THE CROW FAMILY

The crow family (Corvidae) has about 100 species, including the crows, ravens, rooks, choughs, jays, and magpies. Its members inhabit all parts of the world except the polar regions, New Zealand, and parts of Polynesia. Apart from the colourful jays and the piebald magpies, the Corvidae are nearly all black, sinister-looking birds, and many superstititions have grown up around them. Ravens, particularly, are believed to be bringers of bad luck—although it is said of the ravens at the Tower of London that misfortune will follow if they ever fly away.

Jackdaws and magpies are notorious 'thieves'—they will seize any bright object and carry if off to their nests. Both these birds have often been tamed. The whole family make excellent mimics.

The crimson rosella or parakeet is found in
Australia. It uses its curved beak to help it climb.

PARROTS

Most people think of parrots (family Psittacidae) as brightly coloured birds that sit on
perches and repeat what the sailors who
trained them used to say in moments of
stress. In their homes in the wild, parrots
lead very different lives. They live in large,
noisy flocks, and the tropical forests ring
with their cries and glow with their bright
colours. They live on fruit, buds, and nectar,
and, for birds, have a good sense of taste. But
a parrot's full potential, it seems, is not
brought out by life in the jungle. In the company of human beings, parrots demonstrate a
remarkable talent for mimicry, which they
never use in the forest.

What's in a name?
One of the most
strangely named
birds is the domestic
turkey (family
Meleagrididae).
Turkeys originated
in North America,
and were taken to
Europe in the early
1500s. When the
birds were introduced
to England around
1541 people thought
they came from
Turkey. The French
name, *dindon,*
means 'from India

99

FINE FEATHERS

Birds are the only animals to have feathers. Although they look so different from the scales of reptiles, the birds' ancestors, feathers are made of the same substance, keratin—which is also the material of hair. Feathers grow unevenly on a bird's body. Some parts are well covered, others very lightly protected.

There are several types of feathers. Flight feathers, those on the wing, are called primary feathers when attached to the 'hand' part, and secondary feathers when on the 'forearm'. Contour feathers cover the body. Other kinds include the fine, downy feathers of the breast. The number of feathers on a bird varies with its size, ranging from 1,300 up to 12,000 or more. Birds change their feathers by moulting every year.

How a bird moves its wings in flight.

WING SHAPES

An eagle's broad wings give it enough lift to soar high on rising air currents. The swift's narrow, pointed wings enable it to fly fast yet turn easily. An albatross's long, narrow wings allow it to glide over the sea for weeks on end. The duck's short, wide, powerful wings give it plenty of lift. When it is disturbed on the ground it can rise quickly into the air.

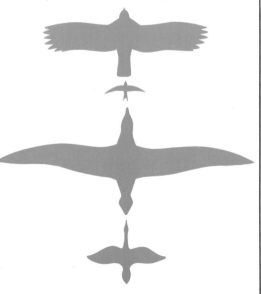

In the world of birds the males generally have the brighter plumage. Many birds are dull in appearance; the best singers are often clad in quiet hues. But tropical birds often show a riot of colour. Among the most ornamental are peacocks (*Pavo cristatus*); the female is a dull, brownish creature, but the male has bright blue-green plumage and a great fan of feathers which he displays when courting. Birds of Paradise (family Paradisaeidae) are also very brightly coloured, and so are many members of the parrot family (Psittacidae).

When the skins of Birds of Paradise first reached Europe in the 1500s from the islands of south-eastern Asia, people exclaimed over their bright colours—and the fact that they had apparently no legs (these were removed before the skins were shipped). The belief that they really were legless, and flew round and round until they eventually dropped dead, is remembered in the species name of the Great Bird of Paradise, *Paradisea apoda* —*apoda* means 'having no feet'!

Above: A young hoatzin. This bird which lives in the flooded forests around the River Amazon, has weak wings and can scarcely fly. Like the ancient Archaeopteryx, young hoatzins have two claws on the tip of each wing, which they use to clamber about in trees.

Left: An albatross glides effortlessly. A heavy bird with weak wing muscles, it needs sustained wind to remain airborne.

101

FLIGHTLESS BIRDS

All birds have wings and feathers and all are descended from flying ancestors. But not all birds can fly today. Where food has been easy to find and there has been little danger from predators, some birds have evolved for life on the ground. Some of these are called ratites, or running birds.

Ratites include the largest bird alive today, the ostrich (*Struthio camelus*). It can run at more than 30 mph (48 kph). A number of large flightless birds live in Australasia. The emu (*Dromaius novae-hollandiae*) is the second largest living bird, males being over 6 feet (1.8 m) tall. The kiwi (genus *Apteryx*) of New Zealand has wings so small that they cannot be seen above its feathers.

The ostrich is the largest living bird; it cannot fly but is a very fast runner.

Above: A gentoo penguin.

BIRDSONG

About one-third of all birds can really be said to sing; scientists do not agree as to why they do it. Singing seems to be mainly defensive, warning others off each bird's territory. It is also often part of courtship ceremonies. But it seems that some birds sing for pleasure; one is the European skylark (*Alauda arvensis*).

Outstanding songsters include the nightingale (*Luscinia megarhynchos*) and the thrush (*Turdus philomelos*) of Europe, the mockingbird (*Mimus polyglottos*) of North America, and the lyrebirds (genus *Menura*) of Australia.

Birdsong has to be learned. Young birds reared away from the company of their own kind never produce the full, true song of the species, and even in natural surroundings it takes some time before birds learn their full repertoire.

The territory claimed by a bird depends largely on the bird's size and on the amount of ground it covers in its search for food. The territory of a Baltimore oriole (shown in yellow) is quite small because orioles do not have to fly far to find insect food. A barn owl eats small mammals such as mice and voles and must therefore cover a far wider area (red).

BEAKS

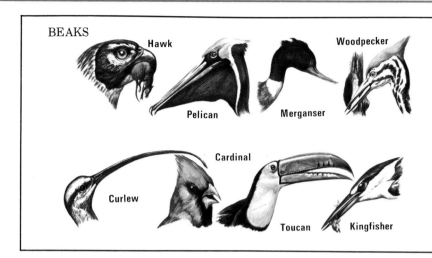

Hawk

Pelican

Merganser

Woodpecker

Curlew

Cardinal

Toucan

Kingfisher

Birds' beaks are adapted in many ways. The hawk's hooked beak can tear prey apart, while the pelican's bill acts like a fishing net. The merganser, a duck, has a saw-edged bill to hold slippery fish. The woodpecker can bore holes and the curlew probes the mud. The cardinal, a seed eater, has a short, strong bill. The toucan can pluck food through foliage, while the kingfisher snatches fish as it dives into the water.

A pair of black swans and their cygnets, which start life pale but darken with age. Black swans live in Australia an have been introduced to New Zealand.

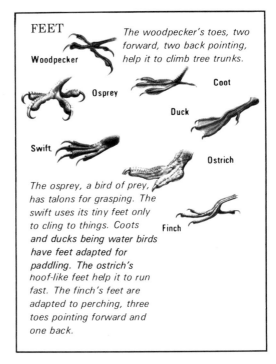

FEET

The woodpecker's toes, two forward, two back pointing, help it to climb tree trunks.

Woodpecker

Osprey

Coot

Duck

Swift

Ostrich

Finch

The osprey, a bird of prey, has talons for grasping. The swift uses its tiny feet only to cling to things. Coots and ducks being water birds have feet adapted for paddling. The ostrich's hoof-like feet help it to run fast. The finch's feet are adapted to perching, three toes pointing forward and one back.

BIRD RECORDS
Largest bird is the ostrich (*Struthio camelus*) of Africa and Arabia. Male birds can stand up to 8 feet (2.45 m) tall, and weigh up to 345 lb (155 kg).
Smallest bird is the bee humming-bird (*Mellisuga helenae*), which lives in Cuba. It has a total length of 2 inches (5 cm), including its tail and its long bill. It weighs about 1/10 ounce (2.8 g).
Longest wing-span is that of the Wandering albatross (*Diomedea exulans*), which can be more than 10 feet (3 m).
Fastest fliers in level flight are probably the swifts (family Apodidae), which can reach speeds of up to 100 mph (160 kph).
Rarest bird may be the Mauritius kestrel (*Falco punctatus*). It lives in thick forests, which are rapidly being cleared to plant sugar-cane. Only two pairs are left in the wild.

Order	Common name	No. species	Examples grouped in families
Passeriformes	Perching birds; passerines	5,000	By far the biggest bird group, including sparrows, weavers; finches; tanagers, buntings; orioles; woodwarblers; honeycreepers; vireos; white-eyes; flowerpeckers; sunbirds; honeyeaters; starlings; shrikes; waxwings; wagtails, pipits; accentors; thrushes, flycatchers; wrens; mockingbirds; dippers; leaf-birds; bulbuls; nuthatches; treecreepers; tits, chickadees; bowerbirds; birds of paradise; wattlebirds; crows, jays, magpies; drongos; swallows, martins; larks; scrub-birds; lyrebirds; asitys; pittas; plantcutters; manakins; cotingas; tapaculos; antbirds; ovenbirds; wood-creepers; broadbills.
Piciformes	Woodpeckers and relatives	400	Also barbets; toucans; honey-guides; jacamars; puffbirds.
Coraciformes	Kingfishers and relatives	190	Also kookaburras; hornbills; todies; motmots; bee-eaters; rollers; hoopoes.
Coliformes	Mousebirds	6	Also called colies.
Trogoniformes	Trogons	36	Single family. Tropical.
Apodiformes	Swifts and relatives	387	Also crested swifts; hummingbirds.
Caprimulg-iformes	Nightjars and relatives	94	Also frogmouths; potoos; owlet-frogmouths; oilbird.
Strigiformes	Owls	130	Barn owls; Strigid owls.
Cuculiformes	Cuckoos and relatives	147	Also roadrunners; turacos, plantain-eaters.
Psittaciformes	Parrot family	315	Also includes parakeets, macaws, cockatoos, lories, budgerigars.
Columbiformes	Pigeons and relatives	305	Also doves; sandgrouse.
Charadri-iformes	Gulls and relatives (mainly waders)	295	Also auks; skimmers; terns; skuas; sheathbills; seedsnipes; pratincoles, coursers; stonecurlews, thick-knees; crab plover; phalaropes; avocets, stilts; sandpipers; plovers; oystercatchers; painted snipes; jacanas.
Gruiformes	Cranes and relatives	197	Also trumpeters; mesites; bustard or button quails; limpkin; rails, moorhens, coots; finfoots; seriamas; kagu; sun bittern; bustards.

Order	Common name	No. species	Examples grouped in families
Galliformes	Game birds	151	Fowl, partridge, pheasant; guineafowl; turkeys; grouse, capercailie; curassows; megapodes, malee fowl; hoatzin.
Falconiformes	Birds of prey	271	Falcons; osprey; eagles, hawks, Old World vultures; American condors and vultures; secretary bird.
Anseriformes	Ducks and relatives	148	Also geese, swans; screamers.
Ciconiiformes	Storks and relatives	120	Also shoebill; hammerhead; ibises, spoonbills; flamingoes; herons; boat-billed heron.
Pelecani-formes	Pelicans and relatives	59	Also tropic birds; cormorants, shags; darters; gannets, boobies; frigatebirds.
Procellari-iformes	Albatrosses and relatives	91	Also shearwaters, fulmars; storm-petrels; diving petrels.
Sphenisc-iformes	Penguins	18	Examples of species: king; emperor; jackass; Adelie. All flightless.
Gaviformes	Divers	5	Also called loons.
Podiciped-iformes	Grebes	21	Examples of species: little grebe; great crested grebe.
Tinamiformes	Tinamous	50	Example of species: little tinamou of Brazil.
Casuariiformes	Emu and cassowaries	4	Single family of Australasian giant flightless birds.
Rheiformes	Rheas	2	Single family of giant flightless birds from South America.
Struthion-iformes	The ostrich	1	The world's largest living bird, living in Africa.
Apteryg-iformes	Kiwis	3	Small flightless New Zealand birds related to extinct giant moas.

A woodpecker finch uses a twig as a tool with which to extract an insect from bark.

Mammals

Mammals, like birds, arose from the reptiles. Mammals are even better adapted to life on land than their reptile ancestors. Like birds, mammals are warm blooded — they can keep the temperature of their bodies steady despite variations in the temperature of their surroundings. They do this by several means, including their warm covering of hair.

All mammals feed their young on milk from their mammary glands. Most retain their unborn young inside their bodies for a period of development, although a few mammals, the Monotremes, lay eggs like reptiles.

Part of a large flock of sheep on a drive in New South Wales, Australia. Sheep are among the ungulate mammals long domesticated by man, and known collectively as cattle. Other cattle include the closely related goats, and bovines.

This animal is a marsupial which looks rather like a mouse but feeds on meat and insects. It was first found in South Australia in 1974 and has not yet been named.

The basic mammal type is an animal with four legs, breathing air, having warm blood, and giving birth to live young. But there are exceptions to this. In seals, for example, the legs have become flippers. Whales also have flippers, but only one pair: they have no hind limbs at all. But the skeleton of a whale has a definite relationship to other mammals—in the flippers are digital bones similar to those of an ape's hand, though greatly changed in size and proportion. A whale has other features common to all mammals—such as lungs, a four-chambered heart, and a well-developed brain.

The two forms of mammals least like the basic type are the primitive monotremes and marsupials. Monotremes—the Duck-billed platypus, for example—lay eggs, like reptiles, but are mammals in all other respects. Marsupials (kangaroos and wallabies, for example) give birth to live young, but only partly developed. The babies spend some time in the pouch on their mother's abdomen.

There are about 4,000 species of mammals, grouped into 19 orders and about 120 families.

Right: A cow suckles its calf. All mammals suckle their young.

Left: A white stoat. In northern latitudes the stoat's fur changes from brown to white in winter, possibly for camouflage in snowy weather.

Below: Dolphins are marine mammals; their limbs have modified to flippers. They are streamline for life in water, and have almost no hair.

The feet of mammals vary greatly, largely according to how much they climb, walk, or run. Bears and monkeys stand on the whole foot, from the toes to the heel. Members of the dog and cat families stand and run only on their toes. The foot is greatly elongated, so that the heel appears to come a long way up the leg. All these animals have five toes. But in the last adaptation the number of toes decreases. The ungulates, such as antelopes, pigs, horses, and cows, stand right on the tips of their toes, and often do not have all five. For example, the rhinoceros has three toes, the camel two, and the horse only one. The nail on the horse's single toe has become greatly enlarged to form a hoof. The cloven hoof of pigs and cattle is really two separate toes. The ungulates include all the mammals with horns; they are all plant-eaters.

MAN AS A MAMMAL
Man is one of the mammals. He has the scientific name *Homo sapiens*. He is the only surviving species of a number of human species that have existed during the past 2,800,000 years. The various living races of Man are all varieties of *Homo sapiens*.

Below: Skeletons of mammalian feet. Horses, sheep (1) and antelope stand on their hoofs or 'nails', the dog on its toes (2), and Man on the sole of his foot (3). The number of toes among the mammals varies. The elephant has five (4), the rhinoceros (5) three, the ox (6) is cloven-hoofed, having two toes, the horse (7) is single-toed, and the pig (8) has four toes.

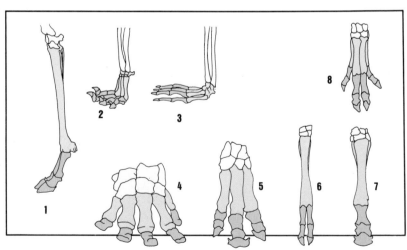

MAMMAL RECORDS

Largest mammal is the Blue whale (*Balaenoptera musculus*), which can be up to 100 feet (30 m) in length.

Largest land mammal is the African elephant (*Loxodonta africana*), which can be up to 11½ feet (3.5 m) tall and weigh up to 7 tonnes.

Smallest mammal is Savi's pygmy shrew (*Suncus etruscus*), which has a head and body length of 1½ inches (3.8 cm) and a tail about 1 inch (2.5 cm) long. Its weight is less than one-tenth of an ounce (2.8 g).

Fastest mammal is the cheetah (*Acinonyx jubatus*), which over a short distance can reach 65 mph (105 kph).

Tallest mammal is the giraffe (*Giraffa camelopardalis*), which can be as much as 18 feet (5.5 m) tall, with hooves 6 inches (15 cm) high, and weigh up to 1 tonne.

Rarest mammals include several species on the verge of extinction, such as the Tasmanian wolf (*Thylacinus cynocephalus*), Leadbeater's possum (*Gymnobelideus leadbeateri*), and the Javan rhinoceros (*Rhinoceros sondaicus*).

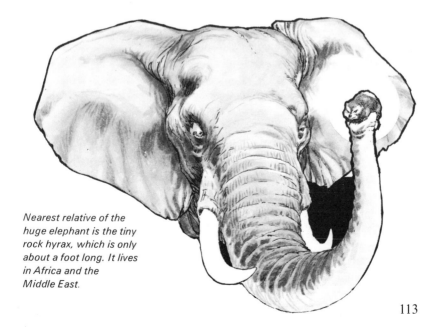

Nearest relative of the huge elephant is the tiny rock hyrax, which is only about a foot long. It lives in Africa and the Middle East.

113

Marsupials

Below: The kangaroo, like most marsupials, has its pouch at the front. The young 'joey' still uses the pouch even when half the size of its mother. The wombat's pouch opens backwards so that it escapes the showers of earth this burrowing animal digs up.

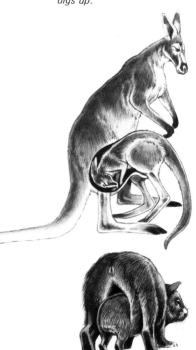

A marsupial is an animal with a *marsupium*—that is a pouch in which the mother can carry her young. Marsupials were common in many parts of the world about 100 million years ago, when dinosaurs were still roaming the Earth. But they died out everywhere except Australia, New Guinea and some neighbouring islands, and in South America.

The reason? Australia, New Guinea, and South America were isolated from the rest of the world for millions of years. More advanced mammals did not develop to compete with marsupials. Eventually, South America joined up with North America, and one species of the South American marsupials moved north. Americans call these marsupials possums.

Ordinary mammals produce fully developed young, even though they are small and helpless. But marsupial babies are minute and only partly formed. They have just enough strength for the most difficult journey they will ever make—over their mother's abdomen and into her pouch. There they stay, suckling on teats, until they are big enough to venture into the world outside.

Most marsupials have their pouches opening forward. Some which dig burrows or live in dense vegetation have the pouches opening backwards so that the soil and other rubbish will not get in.

There are about 250 species of marsupials. Many of them are the equivalents of ordinary mammals in other parts of the world. For example, there are marsupials similar to dogs, cats, mice, rats, moles, badgers, and squirrels—but they have evolved quite independently! But there are marsupials that are uniquely shaped, such as kangaroos.

MAMMALS THAT LAY EGGS

When explorers from Australia brought the first skins of the Duck-billed platypus back to Europe, zoologists just could not believe their eyes. They thought a mammal with a beak like a duck must be a fake. And when people reported that these strange beasts laid eggs —that was too much! But it is true. The platypus is one of a group of animals called *monotremes*, because they have only one opening—a cloaca—at the end of their digestive and reproductive systems, like birds and reptiles. But like true mammals they have hair and mammary glands and suckle their young.

The Duck-billed platypus is a water-living monotreme—it lays eggs and then suckles the young when they hatch.

CAT AND MOUSE

Among the marsupial 'duplicates' are marsupial cats, or quolls as the Aborigines call them. These 'cats' hunt marsupial rats—which look very like ordinary rats—and marsupial mice. Unlike other marsupials, some of these 'rats' and 'mice' do not have pouches in which to carry their young.

115

Left: A young wallaby. These animals resemble miniature kangaroos, but unlike their larger relations their numbers have fallen steeply during this century.

A bandicoot is a little marsupial that looks a bit like a cross between a rat and a kangaroo. It hunts through the undergrowth for insects and worms, and makes a noise like a squeak with a sneeze in it. There are 20 species of bandicoots, and they are between 15 inches and 30 inches (38 cm-76 cm) long.

Wombats are sometimes called 'badgers' because they are something like a badger in shape and size. Some people call them living bulldozers. These chunky animals, up to 3 feet (1 m) long, dig huge burrows with a maze of tunnels. They like to live on their own.

Wallabies are cousins of the kangaroos. They are smaller, the biggest being only half as large as a kangaroo. The Nail-tailed wallaby swings its arms round like windmills when it is bounding along, and has a nail-like tip to its tail. Tree kangaroos are small wallabies that climb trees. They live in the forests of New Guinea and northern Queensland.

Kangaroos are the best-known of the marsupials. They have only one young at a time. But soon after giving birth a mother kangaroo conceives again. The new baby develops a little way and then stops. It is kept in reserve, and as soon as the first 'joey' becomes independent or dies development starts again.

A Red kangaroo stands about 5 feet (1.5 m) tall, but its baby at birth measures only ¾ inch (2 cm) long.

Left: The koala rides on its mother's back for six months after leaving the pouch. Koalas — also called cullawines, buidelbeers, bangaroos, koolewongs and narnagoons — eat only eucalyptus leaves.

An opossum. These little animals live in the Americas from Canada to the Argentine and are the only marsupials outside Australasia.

PLAYING POSSUM

The Virginia opossum, one of 70 American species of opossum, pretends to be dead when attacked. From this comes the popular phrase 'playing possum'. Virginia opossums are found from Canada to Argentina. They prefer to live in trees, but in treeless areas they burrow into the ground. The female carries her babies around on her back after they leave the pouch.

MARSUPIAL RECORDS

Largest marsupial is the Red kangaroo (*Macropus rufus*). Its body is about 5 feet (1.5 m) long, and its tail may be up to 3 ft 6 in (1.07 m) long. It is also the fastest, and can bound along at more than 30 mph (48 kph) for short distances.

Smallest marsupial is the planigale, a kind of marsupial mouse. It is about 3½ in (9 cm) long, including the tail.

Most fussy eater is the koala. It lives only on the leaves of eucalypt trees—and only on the leaves of five out of the 350 species of eucalypt at that!

Least thirsty marsupial is the mulgara, or Crest-tailed marsupial mouse. It gets all its moisture from the insects it eats, and needs no drinking water.

Insect-Eaters

A rare sight — the common, or garden, mole does not show itself very often at the surface. Mole are insectivores that live almost entirely on a diet of earthworms, which they encounter continually in their life of burrowing.

Insectivores are the most primitive of the placental mammals — those that give birth to fully developed young. They are mostly small animals and include such familiar types as shrews and hedgehogs.

Hedgehogs (family Erinaceidae), are animals with a forest of prickly spines all over their backs and sides. Muscles enable the hedgehog to erect its spines for defence.

True shrews (family Soricidae) are small animals which work and rest on a three-hour shift pattern, day and night. Their unpleasant taste keeps them safe from most predators.

Tenrecs (family Tenrecidae) live on the island of Madagascar, and some have been taken to Réunion and Mauritius.

Otter shrews (family Potamogalidae) live in Africa. They swim like otters, feeding on fish.

Elephant shrews (family Macroscelididae) are also called Jumping shrews, because they jump like jerboas. But they have long, trunk-like snouts. They live in Africa.

Moles (family Talpidae) are the master burrowers of the insectivores. A mole can dig its way through 45 feet (14 m) of soil in an hour—and in the mating season it can dig through 150 feet (36 m)! Moles' eyes are capable only of distinguishing light and dark.

Golden moles (family Chrysochloridae) are related to ordinary moles, but their fur is a coppery colour instead of the dense black of their cousins. They live in Africa.

Desmans are somewhat like moles, but lead an aquatic life, burrowing into river banks.

The hedgehog may supplement its diet of insects, snails, slugs, and worms, with eggs of wild birds

HEDGEHOGS

Hedgehogs (Erinaceidae) hide by day in thickets, tree stumps, or rocky hollows, emerging at night to snuffle around looking for their food. When attacked, they erect their prickles and roll into a ball. Any attempt to prise the hedgehog open merely makes it roll up even more tightly. Only the fox and badger can beat this defence, by rolling the prickly ball into a pond or puddle. The hedgehog at once unrolls in order to swim, and can easily be killed.

Another defence mechanism is that hedgehogs are largely proof against snake-bite. The European hedgehog (*Erinaceus europaeus*) is known to kill and eat small snakes—and it also varies its insect diet with mice, frogs, birds' eggs, and carrion.

The Pygmy shrew is the smallest mammal.

INSECTIVORE RECORDS

Largest insectivore is the Common tenrec (*Centetes ecaudatus*), which may be as much as 16 inches (40 cm) in body length.
Smallest insectivore is Savi's pygmy shrew (*Suncus etruscus*), the smallest mammal, which has a head and body length of 1½ inches (3.8 cm).

Flying Mammals

Bats are the only mammals that have mastered the art of flying, though several other species, such as Flying squirrels, Flying lemurs, and Flying phalangers, have managed to become successful gliders. The bats form the order Chiroptera, which means 'hand-wings'. And that is literally what bats have—hands whose fingers have become greatly lengthened, and are connected by a thin membrane of skin to provide a wing surface. The thumb forms no part of the wing, but can be used for holding on to things.

The membranes extend from the 'hands' down the sides of the bat's body until they reach the hind limbs, and there is a further stretch of membrane joining the back legs and the tail. Long hooked claws on the back feet enable the bat not only to climb but to hang from a branch or ledge even while asleep.

There are two main kinds of bats. Fruit bats form the suborder Megachiroptera, and all the largest kinds of bats are in this group. The insect-eating bats (Microchiroptera) are generally much smaller. The bats rest by day and come out to feed at night. They use a form of sonar to navigate and the insect-eaters also use it to locate their prey. There are more than 800 species of bats. They are grouped in 17 families, one of which includes all the fruit bats.

BATS THAT EAT INSECTS

The insect-eating bats (suborder Microchiroptera) form the largest part of the bat world, and three out of the 17 families are really widespread. Nearly all of them hunt on the wing, using sonar. Although called insect-eaters, some eat spiders, fruit, frogs, or fish —and a few prey on small birds and other bats. They live in dark places such as caves, and hollow trees.

A long-eared bat, a member of the large family of Vesper bats. The name is short for vespertilionid — 'belonging to the evening', the time when these animals set out on the search for insects.

Above: A Short-tailed Leaf-nosed bat, which lives with vast numbers of its own kind in caves.

120

BAT'S SONAR

Bats of all families have a sonar system built into their brains. When it is flying, a bat emits a rapid series of *ultrasonic* (above human hearing) signals, which bounce off any object in its path. The echo is detected within one-thousandth of a second, thus enabling the bat to take avoiding action even at the last moment. Bats can fly through a maze of wires without touching one, even in the dark.

Bats emit their signals in two different ways. Some send them out through the mouth, and those that do generally have long snouts. Others send the signal through their nostrils, and they have leaf-like projections above the nose. The nose-leaves serve both to focus the signals, and to prevent them from striking the bat's own ears directly. These ears, which receive the signals, are large and mobile.

Bats find their prey, such as moths, with the aid of the sonar. But many moths are sensitive to the signals, and can take swift avoiding action. Even then, the sonar is so efficient that the bat can make a last-minute swerve to intercept a moth that has changed course. Some moths themselves emit signals which 'jam' the sonar—but bats do not interfere with one another's signals, even when thousands are flying at the same time.

Below: A bat sends out an ultrasonic squeak, which is reflected back to enable it to navigate safely.

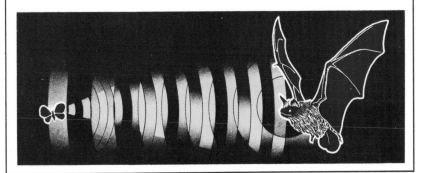

The **Vesper bats** (family Vespertilionidae) are the largest and most widely distributed of the bats. Members of this family are the most numerous bats in North America and western Europe, and there are 275 species. The largest European bat is the Great bat or noctule (*Nyctalus noctula*), with a wingspan of up to 15 inches (38 cm).

False vampires (family Megadermatidae) are often mistaken for vampires—but they do not suck blood! They are found in Africa, Asia, and Australia, and some of them are very large. The Indian false vampire (*Megaderma lyra*), eats flesh, including other mammals, birds, frogs, and lizards. Several American species of the family Phyllostomatidae, the **Leaf-nosed bats**, are also called 'vampires', though some of them prefer the nectar of flowers!

The **Jamaican flower-bat** (*Phyllonycteris*) and the **Long-nosed bat** (*Leptonycteris nivalis*) not only drink nectar but pollinate the flowers, doing the work of bees.

Above: One of over 200 species of Leaf-nosed bat. These animals live on insects, pollen, and fruit which some species are capable of holding in their 'hands' to eat.

Left: A Flying phalanger, a pouched mammal native to Australia. Like Flying squirrels, the phalanger has folds of skin on each side of its body which it stretches out to form gliding 'wings'. The bat is the only true flying mammal.

122

BLOOD-SUCKING BATS

Vampires, according to eastern European legend, are the ghosts of evil men who return in bat-like shape to drink people's blood. Which is why, when real blood-sucking bats were found in tropical America, they were called vampires. They form the family Desmodontidae, and there are three genera, *Desmodus, Diphylla,* and *Diaemus.* They are night-prowlers, seeking sleeping victims for their sole source of nourishment—blood. The Great vampire bat (*Desmodus rotundus*), which weighs about 1 oz (28 g), drinks a table-spoonful of blood every day, from large mammals such as cattle. The smaller vampires suck from large birds.

Above: A vampire bat. It feeds on blood, attacking a sleeping victim so quietly it rarely wakes up. Vampires can transmit rabies.

RECORD BATS

Largest bat is the kalong or Malay fruit bat (*Pteropus vampyrus*), which has a wing-span of up to 5 feet (1.5 m). Its weight is about 2 lb (1.9 kg). It is also called the Flying fox.

Smallest bats are the pipistrelles, several species of which are 3 inches (8 cm) or less in length; they include the European pipistrelle (*Pipistrellus pipistrellus*) and the Eastern pipistrelle (*Pipistrellus subflavus*).

Most dangerous bats are the blood-sucking vampires (family Desmodontidae) of tropical America, because they can transmit rabies and possibly other diseases.

123

Monkeys and Apes

Primates, as their name implies, form the highest order of mammals. They include lemurs, monkeys, anthropoid apes—and Man. But in many ways the primates are not the first among animals. Their physical structure has not evolved so much from that of their basic ancestors as that of, for example, the horse (*Equus caballus*), which has evolved specialized teeth and feet. Primates still have the five-digit hand and foot seen also, for example, in the lowly amphibians.

Above: The potto is a lemur-like primate of Africa. It moves very slowly but seizes its food— birds, lizards, snails, and fruit—with a lightning grab.

Higher primates also have a supple hand with a thumb that can be opposed to the fingers for grasping, and a complex and highly developed brain. They also have eyes set side by side in the front of the head, giving stereoscopic vision. Many of the primates are able to walk erect or nearly so on their rear feet.

Man is the only primate that does not live at least part of the time in trees, and also the only one that does not have an opposable big toe as well as an opposable thumb.

Primates are divided into three suborders:

Prosimii is the most primitive group of primates. It includes the tree-shrews (family Tupaiidae), lemurs, indris, avahis, and sifakas (Lemuridae), lorises and bush-babies (Lorisdae), and the aye-aye (Daubentaridae).

Tarsii contains just one member, the tarsier. This is the only primate which is entirely carnivorous.

Anthropoidea or **Simiae** consists of New World monkeys (Cebidae), marmosets (Callitrichidae), Old World monkeys (Cercopithecidae), and anthropoid apes (Pongidae).

Above: An African bush-baby. It rests by day, but at night it is very active searching for food.

124

PRIMATE OR INSECT-EATER?
Nature sets many puzzles for zoologists who like to classify every living thing neatly. One of those puzzles is the family of tree-shrews (Tupaiidae). These little animals vary in length from 8 to 16 inches (20-40 cm). Most of them look very like squirrels, with bushy tails and long body fur. Their snouts are longer than those of a squirrel, and very far from monkey-like. But their hands and brains are much more like those of the primates, and they can climb in trees in a monkey-like way.

HALF-MONKEYS
Like the tree-shrews, the lemurs (family Lemuridae) come halfway between the insect-eaters and other primates, though they are generally thought to be more monkey than insectivore. The 19 species all live on the island of Madagascar. They have muzzles similar to that of a fox, and large, inexpressive eyes. Most lemurs live in dense forests, but the ring-tailed lemur (*Lemur catta*) likes to live in the open, and spends as much time as it can basking in the sun.

The aye-aye (*Daubentonia madagascariensis*) is closely related to the lemurs. It lives in trees and hunts insects by night.

OLD AND NEW WORLD MONKEYS
The Old World monkeys (family Cercopithecidae) live in the warmer parts of Asia and Africa. They have not spread to Australia, the land of marsupials, nor to Madagascar, where the lemurs reign supreme. They are not found in Europe, apart from the Barbary apes (*Macaca sylvanus*) of Gibraltar—and they were imported from North Africa. There are about 60 species.

Rhesus monkeys (*Macaca mulatta*), like the Barbary apes, are part of a group known as the macaques. Macaques generally are hardy

Right: The squirrel monkey of South American riverside forests lives in troops of up to 500.

125

Above: The male mandrill is one of the most vividly coloured mammals. It is the most fearsome baboon to look at.

creatures, some species living in very cold climates. They are intelligent—in parts of Indonesia and Malaysia the pigtailed macaque (*Macaca nemestrina*) is trained to climb coconut palms and pick only the ripe nuts. Mandrills and drills (genus *Mandrillus*) are among the most colourful monkeys, with bright blue ridges on their cheeks, scarlet noses, and patches of bare skin on the buttocks shading from crimson to blue.

The monkeys of Central and South America (family Cebidae) are distinguished from the Old World monkeys by having nostrils which tend to be wider apart, and by their long prehensile (gripping) tails—a great help in their

Section of a baboon troop, showing how the baboons arrange themselves in 'layers' according to hierarchical divisions. The dominant males (green) and females (tan) with babies (orange) stay in the centre, protected by the outer ring of adolescent males (brown) and subordinate males (grey). Between these two groups the young baboons (blue) are playing. At the bottom of the picture, an adult male is groomed by his mate; grooming is important for the social harmony of the troop.

tree-borne life. Most of the 26 species are not so intelligent as Old World monkeys, and they are much less lively in their behaviour. The most intelligent is the Capuchin monkey. It gets its name from the hair on its head, which looks a bit like the pointed hood (*capuche*) of a Capuchin friar. The only nocturnal member of the Cebidae is the douroucouli or owl monkey (*Aotus trivirgatus*). It has soft, reddish-grey, curly hair. People keep douroucoulis as pets to rid their houses of mice and insects. They can move in absolute silence.

Above: A family of proboscis monkeys. The males develop a long, fleshy nose. These monkeys live near rivers, and swim and dive well.

Noisiest of all monkeys are the Howling monkeys of South America. In the males a bone at the top of the windpipe is enormously developed, forming a resonant sound-box. The howls, which keep other Howling monkeys away from each group, can be heard for miles.

AT HOME

Chimpanzees have a strongly developed sense of social life. They roam the forests in groups, each of which consists of several males and females with their young of various ages. The animals have territories extending over perhaps 50 square miles (130 sq km). At night they build platforms in trees on which to huddle. They are reported to shake hands when meeting each other.

In captivity chimpanzees are quick to learn, both by imitating and by working things out for themselves. A chimpanzee can fit jointed rods together in order to hook food into its cage, or stack up boxes to climb up to a bunch of bananas. Chimps have also been trained to use tools such as hammers and to ride bicycles.

ANIMALS NEAREST TO MAN

Apes are the monkey-like animals that are closest to Man in structure and development. For this reason they are called anthropoid— 'Man-like'. It was once thought that Man was descended from the apes, but it now seems certain that apes and men as we know them today had a common ancestor

Two of the four kinds of apes—the orang-utan and the gibbon—live in Asia, and two—the chimpanzee and the gorilla—in Africa. Remains of the earliest *Hominoids*—the group that includes both apes and human beings—have been found in these two continents.

Anthropoid apes resemble Man in having no tails, and walking upright much of the time. Their brains are much better developed than those of the other primates. Most of the bones, muscles, nerves, and internal organs of apes are very similar to those of Man. But apes have shorter legs and longer arms than human beings, and their big toes are more thumb-like. This allows them to grip the branches and move through the trees at great speed.

THE NOISY GIBBONS

The gibbons (genera *Hylobates* and *Symphalangus*) are the smallest of the anthropoid apes, and the least like Man. Although their brains are comparatively large in proportion to their weight (which usually makes for intelligence), gibbons are not exceptionally intelligent.

Their home is in South-East Asia, from Burma southward to Java and Borneo. They are the most agile of all apes, swinging through the trees with amazing skill. They feed on fruit, shoots, birds' eggs, and newly-hatched chicks. They can walk on their hind legs without difficulty, balancing by holding their arms outstretched or clasping their hands behind their necks. Gibbons are very noisy, and love to howl together.

Below: The skeletons of Man and ape. The ape's arms are longer than its legs and the pelvic girdle (red) has developed according to the different postures.

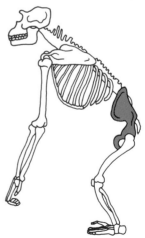

129

An adult male orang-utan, showing his large cheek flanges. His face is almost hairless apart from a beard or moustache.

Right: Guy, a gorilla at London zoo, eating a melon on his birthday — Guy Fawkes day, November 5. Gorillas are vegetarians, feeding mainly on fruit, leaves, roots, and even tree barks.

Below: The comparative brain sizes of Man and ape.

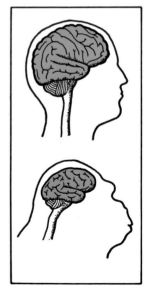

MAN OF THE WOODS

'Man of the woods'—*orang-utan*—is what the Malay-speaking peoples of Borneo and Sumatra call the large, Man-like ape, *Pongo pygmaeus*. The orang-utan looks one of the fiercer primates, but it is comparatively placid, and lives on fruit, leaves, and shoots. When the orang-utan stands upright, its arms are so long that the fingers almost touch the ground. But its legs are disproportionately short. Orang-utans use their long arms to swing through the trees in which they nest. They either live alone or in family groups of mothers with their young.

PRIME PRIMATES

Largest primate is the gorilla (*Gorilla gorilla*). Males are 6 feet (1.8 m) tall, and can weigh up to 450 lb (200 kg).

Smallest primate is the Lesser Mouse lemur (*Microcebus murinus*), whose body is only 5 or 6 inches (12-15 cm) long. It is the fastest-developing primate, maturing at 8 months.

Most intelligent primate, apart from Man, is the chimpanzee (*Pan satyrus*); it is also the best tool user.

Most numerous of primates are the macaques (genus *Macaca*), which live in Asia and northern Africa.

Anteaters and Sloths

Armoured quads
The Nine-banded armadillo (*Dasypus novemcinctus*) is the only edentate which can be found as far north as the United States. It has another unique feature—the baby armadillos are always identical quadruplets. They result from the division of one fertilized ovum into four cells which develop separately. The four babies are, naturally, always of the same sex and exactly alike.

Anteaters belong to an order of mammals known as Edentata, which means 'toothless'. They are the only members of the order that really have no teeth, for the others—the armadillos and the sloths — have teeth. Edentata, in fact, is really a loose grouping whose members are not closely related.

The edentates were a relatively early stage of mammalian development, appearing first about 60,000,000 years ago. Most of them became extinct long ago, but the anteaters, sloths, and armadillos survive in the Americas.

The pangolins (order Pholidota) of Africa and Asia were at one time thought to be relatives of the edentates, because of their habits and lack of teeth. But it is now known that these animals are not closely related to the edentates at all. The termite-eating aardvark of Africa has simple teeth and is also rather edentate-like.

NO BUSINESS LIKE SLOW BUSINESS
There are two types of sloth (Bradipodidae), the ai or Three-toed sloth (*Bradypus tridactylus*), and the unau or Two-toed sloth (genus *Choloepus*). Both eat leaves and fruit.

Sloths are sluggish creatures. Observations suggest that they spend up to 19 hours a day resting, most of that time asleep, and five hours in what might loosely be described as activity. The ai—which gets its name from its plaintive cry—has three toes on each foot, each ending in a claw shaped like the hook of a clothes-hanger. It spends almost all its time hanging upside down in trees, and because it does not move much it is hard to spot. Its coat is green with algae, so it is naturally camouflaged.

Sloths have completely adapted to their upside-down life. Even their fur grows from

their belly to their back, so that rain runs off them easily. On the ground, they have difficulty in moving, but their long, strong limbs are a great advantage when climbing and, surprisingly, when swimming. Unusually for a mammal, the sloth does not have a constant body temperature. The two-toed sloth has the lowest and most variable temperature of all mammals, ranging from 24° to 33°C (75° to 91°F). A sloth's speed increases by half if its temperature is raised by 5°C (9°F).

Above: The typical posture of a Three-toed sloth. It spends almost its entire life hanging upside down.

Class Mammalia: mammals

Family	Common name	No. species	Description and examples
Order Monotremata: egg-laying mammals			
Tachyglossidae	Echidnas	5	Also called spiny anteaters, these are toothless denizens of Australasia.
Ornithorhynchidae	Platypus	1	A furry Australian water dweller with a duck-like bill.
Order Marsupialia: pouched mammals that give birth to little-developed young			
Caenolestidae	Rat opossums	7	Really more like shrews than rats. South American forests.
Didelphidae	True opossums	65	Tree-dwellers that include the only other non-Australasian marsupials.
Dasyuridae	Native cats, Native mice	45	Small or very small marsupials resembling wild cats or mice.
Notoryctidae	Marsupial moles	2	Small marsupials that show a remarkable resemblance to moles.
Myrmecobiidae	Numbat	1	Also called banded anteater. Long, sticky tongue and many small teeth.
Peramelidae	Bandicoots	19	Long, pointed nose—rather rat-like.
Phalangeridae	Koala and relatives	45	Confusingly called possums. Tree-dwellers, some with long tails.
Vombatidae	Wombats	2	Bulky, burrowing marsupials.
Macropodidae	Kangaroos and wallabies	52	Large, medium and small-sized hopping and leaping marsupials.
Order Insectivora: insect- and worm-eating mammals; rather primitive			
Soricidae	Shrews	200	Widespread, small, long nosed.
Macroscelididae	Elephant shrews	14	African, rat-sized, very long nosed.
Potamogalidae	Otter shrews	3	Like miniature otters.
Solenodontidae	Solenodons	2	Ungainly, very long nosed, up to $\frac{1}{2}$ metre long. Haiti and Cuba.
Tenrecidae	Tenrecs	20	Some shrew-like, others hedgehog-like.
Erinaceidae	Hedgehogs	15	Long nosed, prickly coat, widespread.
Talpidae	Moles, desmans	19	Velvety fur, burrowing, worm-eaters.
Chrysochloridae	Golden moles	20	African moles, very like above but with golden or violet-coloured fur.
Order Chiroptera: bats: flying mammals			
Pteropodidae	Fruit bats, flying foxes	130	Large, tropical fruit-eaters, not closely related to other bats.
Vespertilionidae	Typical small bats	275	Includes the pipistrelle, noctule and many other little insect-eaters.
Myzopodidae	(see right)	1	The Madagascar disc-winged bat.
Thyropteridae	(see right)	2	South American disc-winged bats.
Furipteridae	Smoky bats	2	Little funnel-eared S. American bats.
Natalidae	(see right)	15	Funnel-eared bats similar to above.

134

Family	Common name	No. species	Description and examples
Order Chiroptera: bats: flying mammals			
Rhinopomatidae	Mouse-tailed bats	4	Long, thin, mouse-like tail. Old World.
Emballonuridae	Sheath-tailed bats	50	The Egyptian tomb bat, and relatives.
Noctilionidae	Bulldog bats	2	Long wings and pug-like faces.
Nycteridae	Slitfaced bats	10	Peculiar furrow from nose to forehead.
Rhinolophidae	Horseshoe bats	50	Horseshoe-shaped nose. European.
Hipposideridae	Leaf-nosed bats	100	Relatives of above, with similar strange, fleshy nose adornments.
Phyllostomatidae	(see right)	100	American leaf-nosed bats.
Desmodontidae	Vampires	3	South American blood-drinkers.
Megadermatidae	False vampires	5	Leaf-nosed bats (do not drink blood).
Mystacinidae	(see right)	1	The New Zealand short-tailed bat.
Molossidae	(see right)	80	Mastiff or free-tailed bats. Tropical.
Order Primates: tree shrews, lemurs, tarsiers, monkeys, apes, man			
Tupaiidae	Tree shrews	20	Very like insectivores. Tropical Asia.
Lemuridae	Lemurs	19	Madagascar primates.
Daubentoniidae	Aye-aye	1	Rare, spidery-fingered. Lemur-like grub-eater of Madagascar.
Lorisidae	Bush babies and relatives	11	Includes also the pottos and lorises of tropical forests.
Tarsiidae	Tarsiers	3	Small, huge-eyed leapers. Asian.
Callitrichidae	Marmosets and relatives	21	Also tamarins. Very small monkeys of South America.
Cebidae	New World monkeys	26	Spider monkeys, douroucouli night monkey, howler monkeys etc.
Cercopithecidae	Old World monkeys	60	Nearer relatives of man. Include baboons, rhesus, colobus, langurs etc.
Pongidae	Apes	9	Chimpanzee, gorilla, orang-utan, gibbons, siamang.
Hominidae	(see right)	1	Human beings.
Order Edentata: anteaters, armadillos and sloths			
Myrmecophagidae	Anteaters	3	All toothless with long tongues.
Dasypodidae	Armadillos	20	Covering of horny plates. American.
Bradypodidae	Sloths	7	S. American leaf-eaters, hang upside down from branches by strong claws.
Order Pholidota: pangolins			
Manidae	Pangolins	7	Scaly 'animated pine cones', Old World.
Order Dermoptera: Colugos or flying lemurs			
Cynocephalidae	Flying lemurs	2	*Not* lemurs nor do they fly. Gliding tree mammals of Asia.

Hares and Rabbits

Right: A hare, though very similar to the European rabbit, has longer whiskers and black-tipped ears. A hare never burrows, and when in danger it 'freezes' still.

Hares, rabbits, and their relatives the pikas form the group called Lagomorphs, or hare-shaped animals. Hares and rabbits look much alike, and many hares are known as rabbits—such as the Jack rabbit (*Lepus californicus*). But in spite of this confusion the two kinds of animals do have many differences. Hares tend to have longer legs and ears, and they live on their own on the surface of the ground. Because of this baby hares, called leverets, are born with furry coats and able to see and move around. Rabbits are born in burrows, and are naked, blind, and helpless for the first few weeks of their lives.

The only way Man has found to control rabbits is with a virus disease, myxomatosis, carried by fleas. It was introduced to Europe and Australia in the 1950s, and within a few years had nearly wiped out rabbits over wide areas of both continents. A few became immune and have since multiplied.

Rabbits congregate round a waterhole for a drink. In Australia, where they have no natural enemies, their numbers have increased rapidly.

Rabbits breed at a fantastic rate. It has been calculated that if there were no casualties one pair of rabbits could have 13,718,000 descendants in just three years! Back in 1800 there were no wild rabbits in Australia. By 1900 the descendants of a few pairs taken there by settlers had become one of the country's biggest nuisances.

Left: Pikas, or mouse hares, are short-eared relatives of hares and rabbits. They live mostly on high mountainsides, nibbling the sparse vegetation and sheltering from cold winds behind rocky outcrops.

STAMPEDE
When a rabbit community is disturbed an old buck raises the alarm. He thumps the ground with his hindfeet, and all the rabbits within earshot rush towards their burrows. Even here, they are not always safe. Badgers can use their strong claws to dig up the young.

Rodents

THE GNAWERS

The word 'rodent' comes from a Latin word meaning to gnaw—and gnawing is what the life of rodents is all about. Their four front teeth are specially made for gnawing. They are constantly growing, like fingernails, to make up for the wear. The order Rodentia is divided into four sub-orders, containing about 1,800 species. These groups are:

Bathyergomorpha, African mole rats, a small family of digging animals;

Hystricomorpha, including porcupines, coypus, agoutis, cavies, and chinchillas;

Sciuromorpha, consisting of Kangaroo rats, Prairie dogs, marmots, beavers, and squirrels;

Myomorpha, a group containing rats, mice, voles, and hamsters.

Rodents live in all parts of the world, and in all conditions of climate and topography, from deserts to swamps, and valleys to mountains. They are among the fastest breeding of all animals—a pair of rats, for example, can have almost a hundred offspring in one year. Females can be fertile at 6 weeks old.

The mole-rat's most distinguishing feature is its two pairs of enormous front teeth, used for digging.

Below: A rodent's teeth. Its incisors grow throughout its life, constantly being worn away by incessant gnawing.

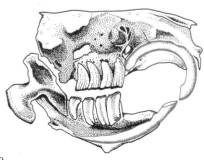

The coypu (*Myocastor coypu*) looks like an outsize rat, measuring up to 24 inches (60 cm) long, plus the tail. Like the chinchilla, the coypu has been hunted for its beautiful fur, known as nutria. It is now bred for this purpose in captivity.

138

RUNNING TO THE ENEMY

The Crested porcupine does not try to escape the enemy by running away. Its tactic is to rush into the attack—backwards with its quills erect. There are two families of porcupines. The Crested porcupines belong to the Hystricidae, Old World porcupines. The quills of these animals lie flat unless the animal is excited. If a spine pierces an enemy, it comes away from the porcupine's skin and stays in the wound, which gradually festers. New World porcupines (family Erethizontidae) are tree-climbers, unlike the Hystricidae which live in burrows, and their diet includes twigs.

Below: Porcupines raise their spines when they sense danger. Very few animals attack them, but some manage to turn the porcupine over and attack its soft underbelly.

Pocket gophers (family Geomyidae) get their strange name from the facts that they have cheek pouches—the 'pocket' part—and that they honeycomb the ground with their burrows—for 'gopher' comes from the French *gaufre*, a honeycomb.

139

MICE

Man has domesticated many animals, but some have domesticated themselves and now live off Man's leavings. This is especially true of the House mouse (*Mus musculus*), which originated in Central Asia but has gone everywhere in the world that people go—some hardy specimens even living in refrigerated storerooms.

The House mouse is only one of several species of Old World mice (subfamily Murinae), which include the Long-tailed Field mouse (*Apodemus sylvaticus*), which lives in gardens, woods, or open country, and the Harvest mouse (*Micromys minutus*), which nests in cornfields in summer and haystacks in winter.

Old World mice accompanied Man to the New World, where there are a great many native species in the subfamily Cricetinae.

A Harvest mouse nibbles an ear of wheat. Its tail curls round vegetation as soon as the mouse stops moving. It is stable even when anchored by only its hindfeet and tail.

Above: The gerbil is a rodent that has adapted to the extreme heat and aridity of desert life. It never drinks, but lives on a diet of dry plant life which its body breaks down to produce water. Gerbils do not sweat thus conserving moisture. Their long hind legs allow them to leap quickly like kangaroos. They escape the heat of the day by burrowing.

A Golden hamster fills its cheek pouches with food, which it carries back to its nest.

The New World mice are anatomically like hamsters, but are very similar in types and behaviour to their Old World counterparts.

RATS

For hundreds of years rats (genus *Rattus*) have been dreaded by Man, because of their destructiveness and their ability to carry disease. Old World rats are relatives of Old World mice, and like the mice they have gone with Man all over the world.

Rats require enormous quantities of food—- a rat measuring 6 inches (15 cm) long and weighing nearly 6 oz (170 g) eats food equal to a third of its own weight every day. That appetite, combined with the rodent's normal need to gnaw to keep its teeth the right length, means that a rat is forever chewing.

Rats breed rapidly. The female gives birth to anything from 6 to 22 young, and within three months those young, if they survive, are in turn ready to breed. If there were no mortality one pair of rats could have nearly 3,000 descendants in a year.

There are two main species associated with Man: the Black rat (*Rattus rattus*), also called the Roof rat because it is fond of climbing, and the Brown rat (*Rattus norvegicus*), slightly larger, also known as the Norway rat or Sewer rat.

Above: The Brown rat (top) although a destructive feeder has a less sinister history than the Black rat (bottom). This carries disease, and the fleas in its fur were the cause of the Great Plague in Europe in the 17th century.

141

Above: The largest rodent, the capybara, and the smallest, the Harvest mouse.

GUINEA PIGS, ETC.

The guinea pig (*Cavia porcellus*), despite its name, is not a pig and does not come from Guinea. It is a domesticated species of cavy from Brazil and Peru, where its wild cousins still live. There are many kinds of cavies in South America, most of them burrowing into the soil to make their homes. The largest member of the family is the capybara, largest of all rodents. Almost as big is the pacarana (*Dinomys branickii*), which lives in the Andes Mountains, and is the sole member of the family Dinomyidae.

A Black-tailed Prairie dog which takes its name from its 'barking' call.

THE TREE SQUIRRELS

There are more than 70 species of tree-climbing squirrels (family Sciuridae), some the size of mice, others as big as cats. The two best known species are the Red squirrel (*Sciurus vulgaris*) of Europe and the slightly larger Grey squirrel (*Sciurus carolinensis*) of North America. In some parts of Europe the Red squirrel is being replaced by the tougher and more destructive Grey squirrel. Among the biggest are the Giant squirrels (genus *Ratufa*) of Malaysia, which have black and yellow coats.

Above: A Red squirrel. It builds a nest or drey of woven twigs lined with moss and feathers.

THE DAM-BUILDERS

Beavers are certainly among Nature's finest engineers. There are two species, the European beaver (*Castor fiber*) and the North American beaver (*Castor canadensis*).

Beavers live in lodges—mounds above the surface of streams; they make sure the entrances to their lodges stay covered with water but the living-quarters are dry by damming the rivers. Their powerful teeth and jaws chew through sizeable trees with the thoroughness of a chain-saw.

Beavers are almost as big as the largest rodent, the capybara. They have broad, flat tails which serve as rudders when they swim. They live on the bark and shoots of trees, and keep a stock of food at the bottom of the stream for winter. In summer they vary their diet with grass, leaves, and buds.

The European beaver was almost extinct by the early 1600s, but has recently been making a recovery. Both it and its American cousin were slaughtered for their fur and for the musk-like secretion, castoreum, contained in sacs near the tail.

Below: A beaver repairs its dam. Beavers fell trees by gnawing through them, and then cut the branches from the trunk and divide them into short pieces.

VOLES AND OTHERS

'A brown little face, with whiskers. A grave round face . . . small neat ears and thick silky hair,' was how Kenneth Grahame introduced the Water rat (*Arvicola amphibius*) in *The Wind in the Willows*. But the Water rat is not a rat at all, but a species of vole. It lives in a burrow close to the water, is a good swimmer and diver, and is mainly vegetarian though it varies its diet with frogs and other small water animals.

The name vole (subfamily Microtinae) comes from the Norwegian *voll*, meaning field, the animal's usual habitat. Voles are stockier than mice and rats, with blunt muzzles, shorter legs and tails, and smaller ears. Some, such as the Northern Red-backed vole (*Clethrionomys gapperi*) even climb trees to find food.

Closely related to voles are the lemmings, famous for their periodic mass migrations, and the musk-rats (*Ondatra zibethica*) of North America.

Below: By eating leaves the Water vole helps keep waterways free of vegetation.

JUMPING RODENTS

There are a number of species of rodents that jump. They form three distinct families.

The **springhaas**, or Cape Jumping hare (*Pedetes capensis*), is the only member of its family, the Pedetidae. It is not a hare, though it is about the same size. It has long hind legs, and resembles a miniature kangaroo, though the tail is bushy. It covers the ground in a series of bounds of up to 18 feet (5.5 m) at a time.

The **jerboas** (family Dipodidae) look like even smaller kangaroos. They live in the desert areas of Arabia and North Africa, and some are found in eastern Europe. The most common species is the Egyptian jerboa (*Jaculus jaculus*), a fragile-looking little animal with a body length of up to 8 inches (20 cm), and a tail that is longer still. The jerboa sleeps by day, bounding around at night to look for food. It is believed to obtain all the water it needs from the plants it eats.

The **Jumping mice** (family Zapodidae) live mostly in North America, though one species, the birch mouse (*Sicista betulina*) is found in northern Europe and Asia, while another group lives in China. The North American species, like their European cousins, tend to live in northern, cooler climates and are most common in Canada.

Overleaf: An albino squirrel clings to the tree with its sharp claws.

The woodchuck, or groundhog, is a large burrowing rodent of North America which hibernates for as long as eight months of the year. According to popular tradition in America, the groundhog comes out of its burrow on February 2 after its long winter sleep. If it sees its shadow, the groundhog takes it as a sign of at least six more weeks of winter weather and retreats into its hole. If the day is cloudy and it sees no shadow, the animal regards it as a sign of spring and stays above ground.

Largest rodent is the capybara (*Hydrochoerus hydrochaeris*), which lives in South and Central America. Capybaras grow to more than 4 feet (1.2 m) long, and can weigh over 120 lb (54 kg).

The largest rat is the Pouched rat (*Cricetomys gambianus*) of The Gambia, which has a body measuring about 18 inches (45 cm) long, and a tail of the same length.

Smallest rodents include the European Harvest mouse (*Micromys minutus*), which has an overall length of less than 2½ inches (6 cm), and some dwarf specimens of African mice which are even smaller.

Class Mammalia: mammals

Family	Common name	No. species	Description and examples
Order Rodentia: rodents, gnawing mammals			
Aplodontidae	Sewellel or mountain beaver	1	Large, primitive, thick-set rodent burrowing in N. America.
Sciuridae	Squirrels	250	Includes chipmunks, marmots.
Geomyidae	Pocket gophers	30	N. American burrowers.
Heteromyidae	Pocket mice etc	70	As above. Also, kangaroo rats.
Castoridae	Beaver	1	Largish, aquatic, builds dams.
Anomaluridae	(see right)	9	Scaly-tailed squirrels. Gliders.
Pedetidae	Springhaas	1	Also called Cape jumping hare.
Muridae	Rats, mice	500	Includes black and brown rats, house mouse; other Old World species.
Gliridae	Dormice	13	Includes fat-tailed dormouse, etc.
Zapodidae	Jumping mice	11	Includes birch mice. Long hind legs.
Dipodidae	Jerboas	25	Very long hind legs for jumping.
Cricetidae	Hamsters etc	570	Also includes deer mouse, gerbil, lemming, muskrat, voles.
Spalacidae	(see right)	3	Mediterranean mole rats.
Rhizomyidae	(see right)	18	Bamboo rats and African mole rats.
Hystricidae	(see right)	20	Old World porcupines. Long spines.
Erethizontidae	(see right)	23	New World porcupines. Shorter spines.
Caviidae	Guineapigs etc	23	The cavy family. South American.
Hydrochoeridae	Capybara	1	Largest rodent; S. American.
Dinomyidae	Pacarana	1	Like a short-nosed, spotted squirrel.
Dasyproctidae	(see right)	30	The agoutis, acuchis and pacas of S. America. Like long-legged guineapigs.
Chinchillidae	Chinchillas, viscachas	6	Thickset with long fur, valuable in chinchilla. S. American mountains.
Capromyidae	Coypus etc	10	'Giant rats' of fairs. Also hutias.
Octodontidae	Degu etc	8	More long-tailed S. American burrowers.
Ctenomyidae	Tuco-tucos	26	Gopher-like but no cheek pouches.
Abrocomidae	(see right)	2	Chinchilla rats of S. America.
Echimyidae	Spiny rats	75	Rat-like, bristly fur.
Thryonomyidae	Cane rats	6	Similar to above, but African.
Petromyidae	Rock rat	1	Squirrel-like African rodent.
Bathyergidae	(see right)	50	African mole rats. Tiny-eyed burrowers with strong digging feet.
Ctenodactylidae	Gundis etc	8	Like guinea pigs but African. Also Speke's pectinator.
Order Lagomorpha: rabbits, hares and pikas			
Leporidae	Rabbits and hares	50	Includes cottontails, jackrabbits.
Ochotonidae	Pikas	14	Short ears; Arctic and alpine.

Mammals at Sea

Having evolved from reptiles more than 200 million years ago, mammals arose as a group of true land animals. But three groups of mammals have gone back to live in the sea. They still have lungs, and must come to the surface to breathe air.

The Cetacea is an order comprising the giants of the ocean—whales, dolphins, and porpoises. They have adapted completely to a waterborne life, and look so like fish that for centuries people thought they *were* fish. They never come to land, even to breed.

The Pinnipedia, or fin-footed animals, are part of the order Carnivora, the flesh-eaters. They include seals, sea-lions, and walruses. All come to land to have their young.

The Sirenia is an order comprising dugongs and manatees, also known as sea cows. They are all herbivores and completely aquatic.

Dolphin escort
For 24 years ships passing through Cook Strait, New Zealand, had a regular escort for part of their journey—a dolphin. He met the ships at Clay Point, north-west of the entrance to Pelorus Sound, and escorted them across the entrance to French Pass. He then waited for a return ship. He was known as Pelorus Jack. He vanished in 1912 after someone shot at him.

THE WHALES

Whales are the giants of the animal world, ranging in length from the 6 feet (2 m) of the Common porpoise to the 100 feet (30 m) of the Blue whale (*Balaenoptera musculus*). There are two main groups.

Whalebone whales (suborder Mysticeti) have no teeth. Their mouths are filled with horny plates of whalebone or baleen, which act as filters. The whale takes in a mouthful of sea water, squeezes it out through the baleen, and so filters out the plankton on which it feeds.

Toothed whales (suborder Odontoceti) include Bottlenosed whales, narwhals, dolphins, porpoises, and Sperm whales, the giants of the group, which measure up to 63 feet (20 m) long. They all eat mainly squid and fish, although Sperm whales may eat larger marine animals such as seals. Male narwhals have a long twisted tusk, which was once widely sold as a unicorn's horn.

PORPOISES

Porpoises (family Delphinidae) are small blunt-nosed sea-mammals that are frequently confused with dolphins. The Common porpoise (*Phocaena phocaena*) lives in the North Atlantic, and is often found near the coasts of North America, the British Isles, and continental Europe. It feeds on herring, sardines, and other small fish—and has 100 teeth with which to chew them! Porpoises grow almost 6 feet (2 m) long, and the females give birth to calves which are almost half their own length.

FINS FOR FEET

The pinnipeds or fin-footed animals spend almost all their lives in water, but they have evolved legs with fins on the ends rather than true fins, like the whales. They can shuffle around on shore, and breed on beaches in great colonies known as rookeries. At breeding time the bulls arrive first on the beaches and stake out territories. When the females swim ashore each bull gathers a harem of up to 50 around him, fighting off any other male who tries to poach either one of his wives or any territory.

There are 32 species of pinnipeds, forming three groups:

Eared seals (family Otariidae) include the sea-lions, the most playful and agile of the seals, and the fur seals, which are still hunted for their lovely coats.

True seals (Phocidae) have no outer ears. Their rear flippers are useless on land, so they pull themselves along with their front limbs. Species include the Common seal, harp seal, monk seal, and the sea elephants.

Walruses (Odobenidae) have no external ears, but they do have hind limbs that can be used for locomotion when they come ashore. Their great distinguishing feature is the pair of long white tusks.

Seal language
Zoologists and seal hunters between them have a special vocabulary to describe sea mammals and their activities. Young males are *bachelors,* and become *bulls* when they mature. The females are known as *cows,* and their offspring are *pups.* A group of young seals is a *pod.* The beaches on which the seals have their nurseries are known as *rookeries.* Seal hunting is called *sealing,* and killing the seals in the water is *pelagic sealing.*

149

Whales have long been hunted and now extinction threatens. Blue whales are now completely protected in Antarctic waters but there are only 2,000 left. Between 1955 and 1963, the stock of fin whales dropped from 110,000 to 35,000.

SEA MAMMAL RECORDS
Largest sea mammal is the Blue whale (*Balaenoptera musculus*), which is also the largest animal. Maximum size is more than 100 feet (30 m) long. **Largest pinnipeds** are the sea elephants (*Mirounga leonina* and *M. angustirostris*). Males grow up to 22 feet (6 m) long and weigh up to 4 tonnes.

A female Weddell seal with her pup. While feeding the pup she will lose about 300 lb (136 kg). Most of this goes to the pup, who becomes so heavy that it can hardly move.

The female sea elephant grows to about half the size of the male—specimens of which have been recorded at over 20 feet (6 m) long.

A dolphin leaps through the air—just for fun. Dolphins are very playful creatures and may sport about in groups for hours.

CARNIVORES

The name of the mammal order Carnivora means flesh-eaters. However, its members are not the only mammals to eat flesh — for example, pigs, chimpanzees and human beings all do so. Neither do Carnivora always live on a diet of meat. Pandas and binturongs are members that live almost entirely on vegetable food, and many others, including bears, have a very mixed diet.

The most completely carnivorous family of carnivores is that of the cats, although weasels, stoats and martens are also great flesh-eaters. The teeth of these animals are beautifully adapted for stabbing, tearing and slicing — but not for chewing. This is the basic carnivore pattern.

The quiet dignity of a resting lioness. Lions and lionesses spend a great deal of their time simply lazing in the sun or shade. They and their lively cubs make up the only large family groups among the cats.

The Weasel Family

The weasel family, Mustelidae, contains not only the weasels and stoats, but also the wolverines, polecats, ferrets, martens, badgers, skunks, and otters. The family includes animals with some of the most beautiful furs, including mink and sable. Most members of the family also have a strong and unpleasant odour, which they produce from glands at the base of the tail when alarmed.

Weasels are the smallest members of the family, being only about 8 inches (20 cm) long, with a very slim body. The similar but larger stoat turns white in cold winters so that it does not show up against the snow. The white form of its fur, known as ermine, is greatly prized.

Polecats are similar to stoats but larger. They are voracious hunters, particularly of rodents, and a domesticated form, the ferret, is used to hunt rabbits. A close relative is the mink, a water-loving animal that makes its home in river-banks, eating frogs and fish.

Ermine, the winter coat of the stoat, was for centuries a royal fur, used for trimming the robes of kings and emperors. It is also one of the furs used in heraldry, and is represented as silver or white, powdered with black spots to imitate the black tips to the ermine's tail.

A weasel. This ferocious hunter attacks creatures larger than itself by biting the back of its victim's neck.

Above: An otter and family. When in the water, this master-swimmer shows three distinct humps above the surface—its head, arched back, and tail tip.

Right: The badger is one of the hardest animals to observe; it only emerges from its set at night and then only when there is no unusual noise or scent.

155

Above: When a striped skunk is threatened with attack, it puts on an aggressive display. It stamps its feet and raises its tail over its back to disclose a pair of musk glands. These glands can squirt a foul-smelling liquid up to 10 feet (3 m). Skunks sometimes live in burrows under outbuildings.

BADGERS

Badgers are rather like small bears in build, habits, and behaviour, but they are classed as a sub-family of the Mustelidae, the Melinae. The common badger of Europe is about 3 feet (1 m) long, with a black and white striped head and a greyish body. Each of the body hairs is partly yellow, partly black, and partly grey. Badgers make their homes in sets and are among the cleanest of all animals. They dig latrines away from the burrow. They feed largely on insects and small animals, and share with bears a love of honey and sweet things. The American badger (*Taxidea taxus*) is slightly smaller than the European badger, and has a white stripe down its back. Other species include the Japanese badger (*Meles anakuma*), the hog badger (*Arctonyx collaris*), the ferret badger (*Melogale moschata*) and the honey badger (*Mellivora capensis*).

CIVETS, GENETS AND MONGOOSES

The small family of Viverridae includes some animals that are like long-muzzled cats. All have short legs and long bodies.

Civets are notable for the strong-smelling musk, used for making perfume, which they produce from glands near the tail. Most of the civets live in Asia, but one species (*Civettictis civetta*) lives in Africa. Like the Indian civet (*Viverra zibetha*), it is a large grey animal which hunts by night.

Genets are similar to civets. They are cat-like in the way they climb and stalk their prey. They produce little or no scent. All but one of the nine species are confined to Africa.

Mongooses are famous for their ability to attack and kill snakes. The Indian mongoose (*Herpestes edwardsi*) was made famous by Rudyard Kipling in his story 'Rikki-tikki-tavi'. The largest of the species is the Egyptian mongoose or ichneumon (*Herpestes ichneumon*), which is more than 3 feet (1 m) long.

The spotted hyaena has a large head and shoulders, and very powerful jaws. It has been known to bite off the iron tongue of a trap.

THE LAUGHING HYAENA

Hyaenas (family Hyaenidae) have a bad reputation as cowardly, ugly animals. This is partly because they eat the left-overs of bigger predators such as lions. But like all scavengers hyaenas perform a useful function, helping to clear up meat that would otherwise turn rotten.

There are four species. The largest is the Spotted hyaena (*Crocuta crocuta*), about as large as a wolf, which lives in Africa. The Striped hyaena (*Hyaena hyaena*) lives in central Africa, south-western Asia, and India, while the Brown hyaena (*Hyaena brunnea*) lives only in southern Africa. The Spotted hyaenas are renowned for the hysterical laughing sound they make, and for the fact that they hunt at night in packs, killing their own food as well as scavenging. The other two species are solitary animals.

The aardwolf (*Proteles cristatus*) is not a wolf at all, but a variety of hyaena. This southern African animal forms a subfamily all on its own, the Protelinae. live mostly on termites and other insects, and occasionally eat carrion. Their jaws and teeth are very weak compared with those of the other hyaenas.

Largest member of the weasel family is the wolverine (*Gulo luscus*), which is 4 feet (1.2 m) long, including a 12 inch (30 cm) tail.

Smallest weasel is the Least weasel (*Mustela rixosa*), of North America, which is less than 3 inches (20 cm) long.

Largest hyaena is the Spotted or Laughing hyaena (*Crocuta crocuta*), which may have a body length of 4 feet 6 inches (1.4 m), with a short tail.

Cats

*Members of the cat family.
Back row: Tiger and lion.
Front row: Domestic cat, wild
cat, caracal, lynx, black
panther, and snow leopard.*

Cats are the most purely carnivorous of carnivores. They have teeth for stabbing and slicing, but not for chewing. Their lithe bodies are built for speed, and their sharp claws are further formidable weapons. Except for differences in size, all kinds of cats are very similar animals indeed. The lioness roaming through the African scrubland is only a larger version of the small cat playing in the back garden. Because of these similarities all cats belong to one family, Felidae, and as they are all meat-eaters they belong to the order Carnivora.

158

Right: The tiger, largest of the cat family, is in danger of extinction.

The cheetah is exceptional among cats not only for its great speed – it is the fastest of all land animals – but also for its non-retractile claws.

159

The cat family also includes tigers, the jaguar, leopards, the cheetah, the puma, the caracal, lynxes, the serval, the ocelot, Scottish wild cats, and several other small wild cats among which are the ancestors of our domestic cat.

Although so similar in fundamental body plan, cats are distinguished by their various ways of life and their calls. Five of the larger cats, the tiger, lion, jaguar, leopard, and snow leopard, are called big cats not just because of their size but also because of their ability to roar.

DOMESTIC CATS

Among the known ancestors of the domestic cat is the Caffer cat of Africa, although the Scottish wild cat may also be an ancestor.

Domestic cats fall into two main groups short-haired and long-haired. Short-haired cats include Burmese, Manx, Abyssinian, and Siamese. Siamese were originally bred in Thailand where they were royal sacred cats. The penalty for stealing one was death. Long-haired cats include the different kinds of Persian and Angora cats. With their long silky hair these magnificent creatures vary in colour from pure white to grey.

AMERICAN CATS

The Americas are particularly rich in cat species, some of which are found nowhere else in the world. The jaguar (*Panthera onca*) of South America is the largest and fiercest of the American cats. It is quite untameable and can attack Man. The puma (*Felis concolor*), also called cougar or Mountain lion, is another cat found only in America. Smaller than these two is the ocelot (*Felis pardalis*) of South America. A beautiful spotted creature, it is also known as the Painted leopard. The American jaguarundi (*Felis jaguarundi*) has a small head and long body.

The wild cat looks much like the domestic tabby cat, but it may be over 3 feet (1 m) long and can kill a young deer.

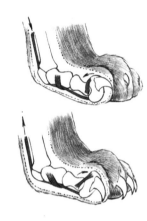

Below: Cats can retract their claws by contracting the muscles to which they are attached.

The Egyptians worshipped the cat. It was called Myeo, which sounds rather like miaow. Killing a cat was a crime punishable by death. When a household cat died, its owner shaved his eyebrows as a sign of his grief.

One story relates that after Moses had opened and closed the Red Sea an Egyptian army commander managed to survive. He escaped to what is now Portugal with his wife Scota, the Pharaoh's daughter, and her cats. One of the couple's descendants became ruler of a northern kingdom which he named Scotland after Scota. With him came domestic cats, descendants of her cats, and the first in Scotland.

REFLECTIVE

Cats cannot see in total darkness, but they can see far better in the dark than Man. At the back of their eyes there is a reflecting layer which sends light back through the sensitive cells so increasing the effect of minute amounts of light on the brain. The layer also makes the eyes shine. A cat's field of vision is exceptional —280°.

Above: Cats were once worshipped in ancient Egypt, and given the same care after death as people. Many cat cemeteries have been found containing mummified cats — and mummified mice.

CAT RECORDS

Largest member of the cat family is the tiger (*Panthera tigris*). Males have been found up to 10½ feet (3.2 m) in length, standing 3 feet (0.9 m) high at the shoulder.

Rarest of the cats is probably the Javan tiger, a race of *Panthera tigris* which is now only known in two restricted areas of the island of Java. About a dozen are thought to survive.

Longest lived of all big cats is probably the lion (*Panthera leo*), which is known to live up to 25 years or more in captivity.

Dogs

Members of a family pack of Cape hunting dogs pose near their zebra kill. They are less closely related to dogs than are wolves, jackals and foxes.

Of all animals, the dog is probably Man's favourite. For thousands of years the dog has guarded Man's home, has herded his sheep and cattle, and has played with his children.

The dog family (Canidae) is quite large. All the members belong to that group of animals known as *Carnivores* or 'flesh-eaters'. The domestic dog (*Canis familiaris*) is the best-known member of the family. There are more than 100 breeds of domestic dogs, ranging from the huge St Bernard to the tiny Mexican chihuahua.

There are quite a number of wild relations, packs of which still roam throughout large areas of the world. The North American coyote (*Canis latrans*) is related to the dog as are dingoes, foxes, jackals, and wolves. Man has occasionally managed to tame a few of these. But there are some wild dogs, particularly in parts of Asia and South America, that have never been tamed.

WOLVES

Wolves, coyotes, and jackals are closely related to the domestic dog. There are two main species of wolf—the Grey or Timber wolf (*Canis lupus*), which is widespread in parts of Europe, Asia, and North America; and the smaller Red wolf (*Canis rufus*), found only in the south-central United States. Wolves are highly intelligent animals which have been respected, feared and hated by Man. Wolves live in packs in which there are strong bonds of loyalty and affection. They also hunt in packs and each family has a clearly defined range in which it hunts. In patrolling their hunting range wolves stop every now and then and urinate on certain trees in order to leave a scent and warn other animals of these territorial boundaries. This characteristic is seen when taking a domestic

The Australian dingo (*Canis dingo*) is a dog with no bark. It is thought that thousands of years ago the dingo was tame and that when prehistoric Man came to Australia, dingoes came with him. Since then dingoes have become wild. Today they roam Australia, either scavenging or hunting sheep.

dog for a walk; its lamp-post halts mark its home ground. Wolves travel widely and although their speed is not fast—they average about 23 mph (37 kph)—they can continue at a loping rate for hour after hour.

Timber wolves are clearly very close relatives of dogs. In fact, the wolf is one of the dog's direct ancestors.

JACKALS
In Africa, parts of Asia, and south-eastern Europe jackals are known as scavengers—they feed on other creatures' leavings. They will even roam villages and carry off human rubbish. But jackals are also fine hunters. Their favourite prey is the fleet-footed gazelle. Either singly or with a mate they chase their prey to tire it and then leap for its throat or belly and tear it with their sharp teeth. What they cannot eat immediately they bury—just like a dog with a bone.

163

Some members of
the dog family. Cynodictis
(1) and Tomarctus (2) are
the ancestors of the others-
—bloodhound (3), coyote
(4), collie (5), cocker spaniel
(6), wolf (7), bulldog (8),
sealyham terrier (9), fox
(10), dingo (11), the
chihuahua (12).

SPORTING DOGS

Gundogs include pointers, retrievers, setters, and spaniels. Such dogs were first bred to find and fetch game.

Hounds include those that track with their nose such as beagles and bloodhounds, and those that use their eyes, such as Afghans.

Terriers include Airedales, fox terriers and sealyhams.

NON-SPORTING DOGS

Utility dogs include various non-sporting dogs that are difficult to classify and range from bulldogs to poodles.

Working dogs include Alsatians, collies, and St Bernards. These dogs were bred for special jobs such as guarding and herding.

TOP DOGS

Heaviest domestic dog is the St Bernard, which weighs up to 220 lb (100 kg) and stands 27 inches (70 cm) high at the shoulders.

Tallest domestic dog is the Irish wolfhound, which is 31 inches (78 cm) high at the shoulders, and well over 6 feet (1.8 m) when standing on its hind legs.

Smallest domestic dog is the chihuahua, which weighs 6 lb (2.7 kg) or less.

Fastest domestic dog is the saluki, credited with up to 43 mph (69 kph), and the greyhound, with speeds over 37 mph (60 kph).

Largest wild dog species is the Timber wolf (*Canis lupus*), which stands 31 inches (78 cm) high at the shoulders and weighs up to 125 lb (56 kg).

165

Bears

Above: A Brown bear. Bears build up stores of fat in their bodies in the autumn and retire to sleep for long periods during the winter in holes under the snow.

Below: Polar bears live on the outer fringes of the pack ice in the Arctic. They are great flesh-eaters; they eat seals for choice, but vary the menu with fish, birds, and walruses.

Bears may look friendly and cuddly; in fact they are among the most ferocious of animals. Although they do not usually attack people, they can be dangerous if provoked. They use their forepaws as their main weapon, either to strike a swift and powerful blow while standing up, or to hug their opponents and crush them to death. A bear's face is completely expressionless, so it is difficult to know what the animal is going to do.

Bears are the biggest of the carnivores and are fairly closely related to the dog, weasel, and raccoon families. They belong to the family Ursidae. Although they look massive and clumsy and have short legs, they can run at speeds of up to 30 mph (48 kph). They can swim, climb trees, and stand and sit upright.

There are several kinds of bears. **Brown bears** live in Europe and Asia. Their close relatives are the large **grizzly bears** (*Ursus horribiliis*) and **Kodiak bears** (*Ursus middendorffii*) of North America. **Polar bears** (*Thalarctos maritimus*) live around the coasts of the Arctic Ocean and are extremely dangerous. The American black bears belong to the species *Euarctos americanus*. **Spectacled bears** (*Tremarctos ornatus*) live in the Andes, while the **Himalayan, Malay,** and **sloth bears** (*Selenarctos thibetanus, Helarctos malayanus,* and *Melursus ursinus*) live in Asia.

THE HONEY BEAR

Most bears have a sweet tooth, and they often have tooth decay as a result! But one kind of bear is so fond of honey that it is often called the honey bear, though it is also known as the Malay or Sun bear. Honey bears live in the tropical forests of south-east Asia. They climb trees to raid the nests of wild bees, without being affected by the infuriated insects.

South America's only bear (*Tremarctos ornatus*) gets its popular name 'Spectacled bear' from the white or tawny markings on its face, which resemble the outline of a pair of glasses. Some Spectacled bears live in dense forest, others in semi-desert regions. The animal climbs trees to gather fruit.

BEAR RECORDS

Largest bears are the big brown bears (*Ursus middendorffii*), which include the Kodiak and Kenai bears of Alaska. They are more than 9 feet (2.7 m) long and may weigh up to 1,650 lb (750 kg).

Smallest bears are the Malay bears (*Helarctos malayanus*), some of which are only 3 feet 6 inches (1 m) long.

Best swimmer is the Polar bear, which is often found several miles out to sea.

Bear wrestling in Turkey.

167

The Raccoon Family

Raccoons and their relatives are North American animals belonging to the family Procyonidae. The Common raccoon (*Procyon lotor*) is about 32 inches (80 cm) long from nose to tail, and has a long greyish-brown coat, much prized by Man for its fur. It swims and climbs trees, and eats almost anything. It is particularly fond of crayfish.

At one time people used to think the raccoon always washed its food before eating. But this 'washing' is just a paddling movement of the front feet, and occurs whenever the animal enters water, even without food.

Relatives of the raccoon include the coati (genus *Nasua*) of Latin America, the kinka-jou (*Potos caudivolvulus*), which has a prehensile tail, and the pandas.

Above: Raccoons are not as sweet as they look. Their nasty habits include robbing birds' nests and raiding chicken coops.

Chia-Chia and Ching-Ching, Giant pandas given by the Chinese to London Zoo in 1974.

PANDAS

There are two kinds of pandas. Strangely enough it is the rarer of the two, the Giant panda (*Ailuropoda melanoleuca*) that is the more familiar. The Giant panda is almost as large as a brown bear, with a distinctive black and white coat. It feeds on bamboo shoots, fish, small birds, and rodents. It is now very rare in the wild.

The Red panda, also called the Lesser or Common panda (*Ailurus fulgens*), is about the size and shape of a large domestic cat, but is closely related to the Giant panda. Its fur is red on the back, black lower down, and it has a white face. It lives in China and Nepal. It eats mainly fruit, but varies its diet with insects, eggs, and even small birds.

UNGULATES

Mammals with hoofs are known as ungulates—from a Latin word, *ungula,* meaning hoof. Ungulates are divided into two main groups: those with an odd number of toes on each foot, and those with an even number. Odd-toed ungulates are the horses, rhinoceroces and tapirs. The more numerous even-toed ungulates include the cattle, pigs, hippos, antelopes, deer, camels and giraffe. Smaller groups of hoofed mammals include the elephants and hydraxes.

Deer are even-toed ungulates.

Elephants

The largest of all animals that live on land is the elephant. Fully grown it may be as much as 11½ feet (3.5 m) tall and weigh up to 7 tonnes. There are two kinds of elephants—the Asian elephant *(Elephas maximus)* and the larger African elephant *(Loxodonta africana)*. Elephants live in herds of about ten to fifty and move quietly through the forests in single file, travelling at about 6 mph (10 kph). Elephants are vegetarian—an adult male may eat about 600 lb (270 kg) of fodder a day.

The elephant belongs to the order Proboscidea, so called because of its very much elongated proboscis or nose. This flexible trunk serves both as nose and hand—it is strong enough to lift a heavy load or deliver a crippling blow, and yet with it an elephant can pick up a peanut or untie a rope. In their upper jaws elephants have a single pair of incisors or front teeth—the tusks. These keep growing all their lives and are used in fighting, and to help lift heavy loads. The tusks are much valued for their ivory, and thousands of elephants have been killed by ivory hunters.

Elephants are peaceful animals and have few enemies apart from tigers. There are amazing tales of the loyalty they show one another; when one is sick the rest of the herd will stay with it until it is well again, and if one is trapped the others will try to rescue it.

RECORD ELEPHANTS
Largest elephant recorded stood about 12 feet 6 inches (3.8 m).
Heaviest known tusk weighs 226½ lb (102.7 kg).
Smallest elephant is the Pygmy elephant *(Loxodonta africana cyclotis)* a variety of African elephant. The males are only about 7 feet (2 m) high at the shoulder.

172

An African elephant, the largest living land animal, enjoys a dustbath. It uses its trunk to spray dust over its body.

Horses and Rhinos

You might not think there was much connection between a horse and a rhinoceros. But they both belong to the same order of mammals, the Perissodactyla. They have hoofs and an odd number of toes—the horse has one toe on each foot, the rhino three. The order contains three families.

The Tapiridae consists of four species of tapirs (genus *Tapirus*), which break the odd-toed rule by having four toes on their front feet. They look like a cross between a pig, donkey, and hippopotamus.

The Rhinocerotidae consists of five species of rhinoceros, of which there are four genera.

The Equidae consists of the horse (*Equus caballus*), the donkey, and the zebra (also belonging to the genus *Equus*).

Left: A Malayan tapir, characterized by the white 'blanket' on its rump. Tapirs are shy, nocturnal animals which eat leaves and fruit. They grunt and whistle, somewhat like pigs.

Left: Zebras drinking at a stream.

Below: The horse, with its single-toed foot, is a mammal that has evolved for maximum forward speed. But very careful breeding by man has produced the racehorse, which has this ability to an exaggerated degree.

Above: A New Forest pony stands protectively over her foal.

ZEBRAS AND DONKEYS

Zebras and donkeys are very closely related to horses, and are in the same genus (*Equus*).

The African wild ass (*Equus asinus*) is the parent stock of the modern domesticated donkey. It is found in Somalia, Ethiopia, and the southern Sudan. It has long ears, brays, and stands just over 3 feet (1 m) high.

The Asian wild ass (*Equus hemionus*) is divided into several subspecies, including the onager of Iran and Afghanistan, the kulan, found near the Gobi Desert of central Asia, and the kiang of Tibet and Sikkim.

Zebras are African animals. Their black and white stripes which appear so conspicuous in fact help them as camouflage in the wild. The species vary in size and in the width of the stripes. Burchell's zebra is the most common, but seven distinct types of zebra are distinguished.

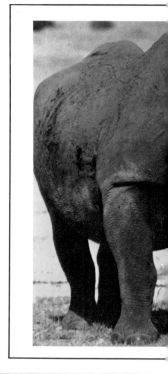

THE MULE

Mules are a cross between a male ass and a female horse. They are tough, surefooted animals, better for work than either parent. Unfortunately most mules are sterile— they cannot produce offspring. They have a reputation for obstinacy which has become a byword.

THE BIG FIVE

The **Indian rhinoceros** (*Rhinoceros unicornis*) is the largest of the three Asian species. It is about 5 feet 8 inches (1.7 m) high at the shoulders, and weighs about 8,800 lb (4,000 kg). It has a single horn measuring about 2 feet (60 cm) long.

The **Javan rhinoceros** (*Rhinoceros sondaicus*) is similar but much smaller. It is very rare.

The **Sumatran rhinoceros** (*Didemocerus sumatrensis*), is the smallest of all rhinos, and weighs about a tonne. It has two horns.

The **White rhinoceros** (*Ceratotherium simum*) of Africa is the largest of all rhinos. Despite its name, it is about the same colour as the **Black rhinoceros** (*Diceros bicornis*), the other African species. They are both bluish grey and have two horns.

Despite its fearsome appearance, the rhinoceros (a name meaning in Greek 'nose-horned') is a placid vegetarian, browsing on leaves and grass. Its horn (or horns) is really a mass of hair fused together which it uses against predators.

Left: Wild asses were once common in India, but there are now fewer than 1,000 in existence. Many have died from diseases caught from donkeys (domesticated asses) and horses.

Largest horse breed is the Shire, which may be more than 17 hands (5 feet 8 inches; 1.7 m) high.

Smallest horse breed is the Falabella pony, whose average height is 7 hands (28 inches; 70 cm).

Largest rhinoceros is the White rhinoceros (*Ceratotherium simum*), over 5 feet 8 inches (1.7 m) tall at the shoulder.

Smallest rhinoceros is the Sumatran rhinoceros (*Didemoceros sumatrensis*) which is only about 4 feet 6 inches (1.4 m) high.

Camels

Camels and their relatives have long been among the most useful of animals to Man. There are two kinds of camels: the Bactrian camel *(Camelus bactrianus)* has two humps on its back, while the Arabian camel, often called the dromedary *(Camelus dromedarius)* has one hump. (Strictly speaking, a dromedary is a racing camel.) The camel is often called the 'Ship of the Desert' because it can go for long periods without eating or drinking. The hump is a reserve of fat on which the animal draws when it cannot feed.

The camel is well adapted to desert life. Its long eyelashes and muscular nostrils keep out the sand and it has a large body surface for easy loss of heat.

Camels have broad feet that pad over desert sands, and nostrils that can be closed against dust. The largest camels can carry loads of up to 450 lb (200 kg) and cover as much as 40 miles (65 km) in a day.

Left: The llama is a domesticated camel relative of the
high Andes of South America.
Its wild ancestor is the
guanaco, which still lives in
the same mountainous
regions.

Camels live in Asia and Africa, and except for some herds of Bactrians in the Gobi Desert are known only as domesticated animals. Their relatives live in South America, where they are known as both wild and domesticated beasts. They are llamas, and there are two main kinds, the guanaco *(Llama huanacos)* and the vicuña *(Llama vicugna).* Guanacos are about 4 feet (1.2 m) high at the shoulder, about two-thirds the size of camels. The vicuñas are smaller and rarer, and are found only in the remote mountains of Peru. Domesticated animals have been bred from guanacos and are known as llamas.

THE ALL-PURPOSE ANIMAL

To the Arabs of the deserts of northern Africa and south-western Asia the camel is truly an all-purpose animal. It is the principal beast of burden, but in addition the Arabs drink its milk, and also eat camel meat. The hair of the camel is valuable and is used for making cloth. Its leather makes dishes and sandals, and camel droppings are dried and used for fuel.

Above: The dromedary is the riding breed of the Arabian camel (top). The Bactrian camel is most suitable as a pack animal.

179

Pigs and Hippos

Right: Two warthogs fight, while a third awaits the outcome. The male has four large warts on its head, which appear to serve no purpose.

Pigs and hippopotamuses, unlike most of the other even-toed ungulates (order Artiodactyla), are not ruminants—that is, they do not chew the cud. They form a suborder (Suiformes). There are two species of hippos, and several kinds of wild pigs.

The wild boar (*Sus scrofa*) roams over wide areas of Europe, Asia, and northern Africa. It is a strong, thick-skinned animal, which can get up quite a speed when pursued. Our domestic pig is descended from the wild boar. There are several related species, including the Indian boar (*Sus cristatus*).

The warthog (*Phacochoerus aethiopicus*) is an African animal—and one of the ugliest. It has wart-like lumps on its face, huge tusks, and a coarse grey skin. In Afrikaans it is called *vlakte-vark*—'pig of the plains'—from its habit of preferring open country.

The babirusa (*Babirussa babyrussa*) of the Celebes has long, apparently useless, curved tusks which give it a ferocious appearance quite unlike its character.

WATER-HORSES

Hippopotamuses get their name from two Greek words meaning 'river-horse', and indeed these huge animals spend a great part of their lives in or under water. On land the Great African hippopotamus (*Hippopotamus amphibius*) is a lumbering, ungainly animal weighing 4 tonnes. Under water in the rivers and lakes where it lives, it can close its nostrils and tiptoe along the bottom with the grace and agility of a ballet dancer. Hippos spend most of the daylight hours dozing, with just their nostrils above the water. They come to land to graze at night. The Pygmy hippopotamus (*Choeropsis liberiensis*), weighing only about 560 lb (250 kg), spends much more time on land.

The hippopotamus (its name means 'river horse') lives in the rivers and swamps of tropical Africa. Closely related to the pig, the hippopotamus is the second largest land mammal. It moves clumsily on land but can gallop at a surprising speed.

Ruminants

Most of the hoofed animals with even numbers of toes—two or four—belong to the group known as the ruminants—the cud-chewers. They have evolved a complex digestive system to cope with their diet of grass and other hard-to-digest vegetation.

A typical ruminant, such as a cow, has a four-part stomach. All the grass it bites off is mixed with saliva and swallowed whole, to be stored in stomach No. 1, the *rumen* or paunch. There the food is heated up so that bacterial action can take place to break down the most indigestible part of the grass, the cellulose. From the rumen the food passes to stomach No. 2, the *reticulum* or honeycomb stomach, where it is moulded into pellets, or cuds. When the cow has finished grazing it lies down and regurgitates the cuds into its mouth, where it chews solidly away for hours to break down the food. The food then goes to the third and fourth stomachs, the *omasum* and the *abomasum,* for further digestion.

ANTELOPE ATHLETES
Antelopes (subfamily Antilopinae) come in a great variety of shapes and sizes. Some are as large as an ox, others no bigger than a rabbit. Some have long horns, others none at all. Some live in forests, others in deserts. They are the most graceful of all animals.

Antelopes are splendid athletes. The springbok *(Antidorcas marsupialis)* of South Africa is the high-jumper of the family; it can leap 10 feet (3 m). The beautiful gazelles are the cross-country champions; they can run for long periods at more than 40 mph (65 kph). Other African antelopes include the eland *(Taurotragus oryx)* of East Africa which has long, spirally twisted horns which it uses to break small boughs when searching for food.

Below: The horns of cattle and antelopes are permanent hollow outgrowths of hardened epidermis surrounding a bony core. They are not branched. The antlers of deer are bony outgrowths, shed each year. These are the antlers of a Red deer; with each year extra tines or points are added.

Asian antelopes include the Arabian oryx (*Oryx leucoryx*), saved from extinction in the 1960s by the establishment of a breeding herd in Arizona, USA by several wildlife societies. The largest Asian antelope is the blue bull (*Boselaphus tragocamelus*), also called the nilghai. The blackbuck (*Antilope cervicapra*) of India is another animal renowned for its great speed. Only cheetahs can catch it.

Above: A Hereford bull. This famous breed of beef cattle originated in Britain and has been spread over all cattle-rearing parts of the world.

The Arabian oryx stands only 3 ft 3 in. (1 m) at the shoulder. It is nearly extinct in the wild but has been successfully bred in captivity.

183

Goats and sheep are very closely related. The domesticated goat—'the poor man's cow'—is descended from the pasang or wild goat (*Capra hircus*) of Turkey. The domestic sheep (*Ovis aries*) has been kept by Man since prehistoric times. Goats are distinguished from sheep by the beard on the chin of most males and some females. Goats also have shorter tails than sheep and they turn up. Goats are usually covered in straight hair but some kinds have a woolly undercoat.

Mountain bighorn rams collide in a contest for dominance. This does the rams little physical harm, but the winner will sire more offspring.

All-purpose yak
The yak (*Poephagus grunniens*) is a cousin of the bison of Europe and America. It is one of the hardiest of all animals, living at anything up to 20,000 feet (6,000 m) above sea level, and has a long shaggy coat that almost reaches the ground. Tibetans use the yak as a pack animal. It provides them with milk, meat and clothing.

Milking a goat. Although goats give less milk than cattle they thrive on much poorer pasture.

DESERT ISLAND

In the early 1600s the Portuguese took a herd of goats to the fertile, wooded island of St Helena off the west coast of Africa. Goats have voracious appetites. They do not simply munch grass, they rip out the entire plant. They tear leaves off trees and sometimes clamber up the branches. More seriously they eat plant seeds and pull young trees out of the ground and so prevent the growth of new plants. Within 200 years, the goats had destroyed most of the plant life of St Helena. In 1810 all the goats were killed, but by then the wind and rain had eroded most of the unprotected soil.

HORNS THAT AREN'T

One of the main characteristics of the true deer (family Cervidae) is that the males of most species have horn-like outgrowths on their head called antlers. Antlers are not horn, but bone, and they are shed and grown afresh every year. An exception is Père David's deer, which sometimes changes antlers twice a year.

There are about 40 species of deer, ranging from the giant Alaskan bull moose to the pudu (*Pudu pudu*) of Chile, which is rarely more than 1 foot (30 cm) high. Red deer *(Cervus elaphas)* live wild in Europe, Asia and northern Africa, and now have been introduced into New Zealand. The reindeer (*Rangifer tarandus*) of northern Europe is the only truly domesticated deer; in the Arctic Circle it takes the place of cattle. The caribou (*Rangifer arcticus*) of America is almost identical, but has never been domesticated. The European elk (*Alces alces*) and the American moose (*Alces americana*) are two other deer that are almost identical.

Below: Moose wading through the water where they browse on lilies and leaves. The largest living deer, the moose lives in the coniferous forests of Europe and Asia (where it is called an elk) and North America.

Above: The sensitive, rather camel-like face of the world's tallest animal, the giraffe of the African plains.

186

TALL, SHY, AND SOFT-VOICED

The world's tallest animals and some of its shyest make up the small family Giraffidae. These animals have short, stubby horns which are actually bony outgrowths with a covering of skin, or bare in the case of the okapi (*Okapia johnstoni*).

Giraffes (*Giraffa camelopardalis*) stand up to 18 feet (5.5 m) high. Their long necks, which enable them to browse on tall trees, have the same number of vertebrae that most other mammals have—seven. Usually silent, they can make a soft, fluting sound.

Okapis are such retiring creatures that they were unknown to science until 1900. The okapi is thought to represent a survival of the prehistoric animals, *Palaeotragus*, regarded as the ancestor of the giraffe.

RUMINANT RECORDS

Largest deer is the Alaskan bull moose (*Alces americana*), which stands about 8 feet (2.4 m) high at the shoulder and weighs 1,800 lb (800 kg).

Largest antelope is the Giant eland, or Lord Derby's eland (*Taurotragus oryx*), which is about 6 feet (1.8 m) high at the shoulder and weighs a tonne.

Largest wild ox is the gaur (*Bibos gaurus*) of India and south-eastern Asia. It stands 6 feet 4 inches (2 m) at the shoulder.

Largest wild sheep is the argali (*Ovis ammon*) of central Asia. It stands 4 feet (1.2 m) high and weighs over 300 lb (140 kg).

Largest wild goat is the markhor (*Capra falconeri*) of Afghanistan, which stands about 40 inches (1 m) high at the shoulders and weighs more than 200 lb (90 kg).

Smallest ruminants are the hornless little chevrotains (genus *Tragulus*) which hide in the forests of India and Indonesia. Some species are only 8 inches (20 cm) tall at the shoulder.

Family	Common name	No. species	Description and examples
Order Cetacea: whales, including dolphins and porpoises			
Platanistidae	River dolphins	4	Long beak-like snouts. Sometimes blind.
Ziphiidae	Beaked whales	15	Medium-sized, dolphin-like whales.
Monodontidae	White whales	2	Includes beluga and tusked narwhal.
Delphinidae	(see right)	50	Dolphins and porpoises. Killer whale.
Physeteridae	Sperm whales	2	Medium or very large toothed whales.
Balenopteridae	Rorquals or fin whales	6	Whalebone whales, including the blue whale, largest of all animals.
Balenidae	Right whales	3	Long-headed whalebone whales.
Eschrichtiidae	(see right)	1	The Californian grey whale.
Order Carnivora: flesh-eating mammals			
Mustelidae	Weasel family	70	Also includes stoats, badgers, wolverine, otters, skunks, mink, martens.
Viverridae	Civets and relatives	75	Also includes genets, mongooses, binturong, suricates.
Hyaenidae	Hyaenas	4	Spotted, brown and striped hyenas and termite-eating aardwolf.
Felidae	Cats	34	Includes lions, tigers, cheetah, leopard, serval, wild cats etc.
Canidae	Dogs etc	37	Includes wolves, jackals, foxes, Cape hunting dog, S. American zorro.
Ursidae	Bears	7	Polar bear; brown bears including grizzly; black bear, sun bear etc.
Procyonidae	Pandas and racoons etc	18	Also giant panda, coati, kinkajou, cacomistle. Eat mixed or plant food.
Order Pinnipedia: seals and walrus, closely related to carnivores			
Phocidae	Seals	18	No external ears. Includes elephant seal, grey seal, leopard seal.
Otariidae	Sea lions	13	Have ear flaps. Includes fur seal.
Odobenidae	Walrus	1	Large, tusked Arctic denizen.

Family	Common name	No. species	Description and examples
Order Artiodactyla: hoofed mammals with an even number of toes			
Suidae	Pigs	8	Includes wart hog, babirusa.
Tayassuidae	Peccaries	2	Small, tusked, pig-like, S. American.
Hippopotam-idae	Hippopotamus	2	Common hippo, weighing 4 tonnes, and pigmy hippo, 300 kg.
Camelidae	Camels	3	Also dromedary, llama, guanaco, vicuna.
Cervidae	Deer	40	Includes red, sika, fallow, musk, Père David's, Chinese water, moose deer.
Tragulidae	Chevrotains	4	Small, primitive deer with tusks.
Bovidae	Cattle and antelopes	110	Includes yak, sheep, goats, bison, buffalo, musk ox, wildebeeste, eland.
Antilocapridae	Pronghorn	1	N. American deer-antelope.
Giraffidae	Giraffe, okapi	2	Giraffe is world's tallest animal. Okapi is denizen of Congo forests.
Order Perissodactyla: hoofed mammals with an odd number of toes			
Tapiridae	Tapirs	4	Nose trunk-like. S. America; Malayasia.
Rhinocerotidae	Rhinoceroses	5	White, black, Indian, Javan, and Sumatran rhinos.
Equidae	Horses and zebras	6	Also Przewalski's horse; wild ass; donkeys.
Order Sirenia: sea cows, water mammals *not* closely related to whales, seals etc			
Trichechidae	Manatees	3	Bulky planteaters. Florida creeks, etc.
Dugongidae	Dugong	1	As above, but Pacific and Indian oceans.
Order Tubulidentata: the aardvark			
Orycteropod-idae	Aardvark (Africa)	1	Not closely related to other mammals. Powerful digger and termite eater.
Order Hyracoidae: hyraxes or dassies			
Procaviidae	Hyraxes, dassies	6	Small hoofed animals superficially like rabbits but more nearly related to elephants.
Order Proboscidae: elephants			
Elephantidae	Elephants	2	The African and Indian (Asiatic) elephants, the world's largest and heaviest land animals, with a unique, prehensile trunk.

The white rhinoceros is not white but dark grey.
Ruthlessly hunted by Man it is danger of extinction.

ANIMAL BEHAVIOUR

Until the beginning of this century, animals other than human beings were considered by scientists, to behave almost entirely by instinct, to have no inner life.

Since that time, a whole new branch of science, called ethology, has arisen to deal with animal behaviour, as it has become clear that animals do indeed have complex and fascinating inner lives. This applies most particularly to the animals with the most advanced brains, the mammals and birds.

Ethologists study the behaviour of animals at all phases of their life, including courtship, mating, nest-building and rearing young. They also study the behaviour of animals in their groups — herds, flocks or family parties.

But these studies cannot really be separated from the external appearance of the animal —for example, a duck 'talks' to a drake, and *vice versa*, by displaying the colour patterns of her plumage. Also, the way in which an animal gets its food is included in its behaviour — a hawk cannot fully be understood without knowing how it hunts, or a sloth without knowing how it browses.

A Little owl returns to its nest with its prey — a night flying moth. Owls are among the most silent of flyers.

Keeping Alive

Above: The caterpillar of the puss moth blows up a section of loose skin on its neck when attacked. The skin forms a mask, with false eyes and a gaping mouth.

In the world of what the poet Alfred, Lord Tennyson called 'Nature, red in tooth and claw', survival is for the fittest animal. Man is the only animal whose weaklings stand much of a chance. In the wild, every animal has to find its own food, make its own home, and escape danger as best it can. Study of fossils shows that many species have become extinct because they could no longer meet the challenge of their environment.

But many species do survive—by adapting to their environment. Sometimes they do it by changes in bodily shape, like the mole, which is designed for tunnelling. Sometimes survival is a matter of not being seen by predators, which is the result of good camouflage. For example, the Arctic hare is brown in summer when the plants among which it lives are brown and green, and white in winter when snow covers the land. But for the most part survival is a matter of being successful in the endless search for food—and if, as with the shrews, an animal eats its own body weight in food every three hours, that hunt for food is a constant preoccupation.

Above: The pangolin, or scaly anteater, curls up for protection. When disturbed it can dig itself completely underground in less than 10 minutes.

COPYSNAKE
The harmless Scarlet kingsnake of the Americas looks exactly like the poisonous coral snake, with distinctive red, black, and white bands on its body. The kingsnake uses its similarity to the coral snake as a means of protection against predators. In the same way some species of hoverflies, such as *Xanthogramma pedissequum*, look uncannily like the dangerous wasp—enough to deter a hungry bird, anyway!

ABANDON CHICKS
It may seem odd to abandon your chicks to save them—but that is just what the ground-nesting Ringed plover does. If a fox or other predator is near, the mother bird draws it away by running from the nest trailing one wing as if it is broken. Once she has gained enough ground she takes swiftly to the air.

Above: A lizard breaks off its tail to escape from its captor. Many lizards can shed their tails in this way, regrowing them later.

LIVING TO TELL THE TALE

Resistance to cold is shown by the 50 or so species of insects, spiders, and other small animals living in Antarctica—which survive winter temperatures of −62°C (−80°F).

Resistance to heat is shown by the goldfish (*Carassius auratus*) which live in the hot springs of Bath, in the west of England, where the water may be at 49°C (120°F).

Longest survival is shown by some of the reptiles, such as the Giant tortoise (*Testudo gigantea*), specimens of which have been noted as living more than 150 years. But those protozoa which reproduce by division are in a sense immortal, as the cell never dies, but splits to form new animals.

Food Chains

Every animal depends on some other living thing for its food. Ultimately, all living things depend on the Sun, whose light-energy enables plants to make their own food. Every animal eats either plants or other animals that have eaten plants.

The food chain begins with plants, which are able to manufacture their own food from water, carbon dioxide, and minerals from the soil. To do this they absorb energy from the sun. This process is called photosynthesis. The plants are eaten by herbivores, animals which live on plants alone, and omnivores, which eat both animals and plants. These are eaten by predators, which may in turn be eaten by larger predators, or by scavengers, which do not kill for food, but eat animals whose dead bodies they find. Every creature dies eventually, and its tissues are consumed by bacteria and fungi.

194

The food chain on a North American prairie. Plants make food using the sun's energy (1). They are eaten by Prairie dogs (2) which are in turn the food of the coyote (3). The coyote itself is preyed on by the Golden eagle (4), whose body after death is food for bacteria (5). The bacteria produce the plant food nitrogen.

THE BALANCE OF NATURE

Unless disturbed by Man, any one part of the countryside will always tend to support the same animals and plants. This ability of Nature to remain unchanged is called the balance of Nature. For example, if a stretch of grassland is able to provide food for a dozen rabbits, then a dozen rabbits will generally be found there. If too many rabbits move in, then there will not be enough food for them all; some will either die or migrate, and the balance will be restored. Similarly, if the grassland becomes overgrown, more animals will arrive to feed on it. The same grassland may provide enough rabbits to feed one fox. If the fox eats all the rabbits, it too will have to move on while the population recovers.

Over long periods there are, of course, changes. Some are cyclic, occurring every few years. For example, every four years the numbers of snowy owls in the Arctic rise to a peak level, then drop back. Over much longer periods, of thousands of years, permanent changes occur—generally due to changes in the climate. For example, the lion, a warm-climate animal, was once plentiful in Europe, where the climate has now become too cold for it to survive.

195

IN THE SEA

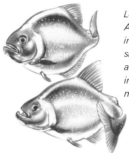

Left: The deadly South American piranha fish. Their instinct to attack where they smell blood is so strong that a large shoal can turn a cow into a skeleton in under five minutes.

In the sea, algae (1) get energy direct from the Sun. They are eaten by the animal plankton (2) which form the diet of herrings (3). These are eaten by larger fish, like cod (4), whose bodies are broken down by bacteria (5).

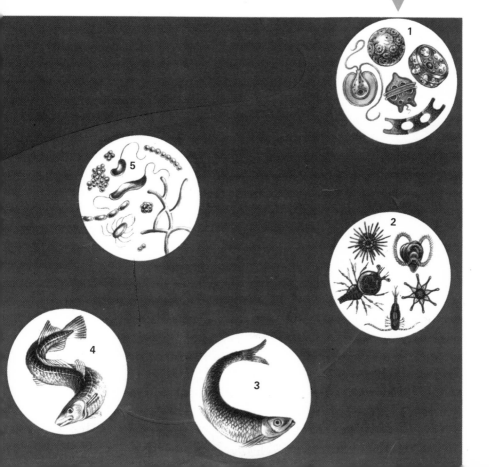

FISH DEFENCE

Pufferfishes (family Tetraodontidae), are shaped for safety. Most of them live in tropical waters. When danger threatens, the fish swallow water and swell themselves up to two or three times their normal size, making themselves difficult for a predator to swallow. The porcupinefish (*Diodon*), a relative of the puffers, is covered with bony spines, and when it swells up its body the spines stand upright, to make it even less edible!

Poison is another weapon of self-defence; some of the brightly coloured puffers found off the coast of Japan are so deadly that they can cause serious illness to anyone who eats them. Probably the most poisonous of all fishes is the stonefish (*Synanceja verrucosa*). It looks very like the stones on the sea-bottom close to the shores of South America, where it lives. Its head is full of hidden spines connected to poison glands. If an unwary swimmer steps on the stonefish the sting can cause terrible pain, and may even kill.

Above: The cuttlefish emits an inky cloud when attacked. This serves as a smoke screen to draw away the enemy's attention while the cuttlefish swims away.

SCAVENGERS

Nature is never wasteful. The dead bodies of animals and plants are food for the scavengers, a huge population ranging in size from hyenas, marabous and vultures to beetles

The marabou stork of Africa eats carrion and refuse; in some places its value as a scavenger means that it is protected by law.

Animals in Disguise

Camouflage is the disguise used by animals to hide from their enemies. Man also uses camouflage, particularly in war, but his disguises are crude compared with those of animals.

Most animals use camouflage to hide from predators, other animals who prey on them. But sometimes the predator itself uses a disguise to hide from its prey.

An animal whose colour matches its surroundings is difficult to see. The white Arctic hare (*Lepus arcticus*), for example, can hardly be seen in the snow. Patterns, too, provide camouflage. Spots, stripes, and other patterns help some creatures to blend into multicoloured surroundings or areas of sun and shade.

Many animal colours are produced by cells in their skin which contain pigment (colouring

The female eider duck's speckled feathers blend with its surroundings to protect it when nesting.

matter). By altering the size of these cells, an animal can change colour to match its background very quickly. The chameleon is a good example among reptiles.

Some animals disguise themselves by looking like something else. This *protective resemblance* is common among insects. A classic example is the stick insect whose long body exactly resembles a twig. Leaves, stones, and flowers are also imitated.

The Indian tiger's stripes imitate the shadows of jungle vegetation.

THROWN BY A VOICE

Most camouflage is a matter of deceiving the eyes of the enemy. Thus the camouflaged animal escapes detection. But the Italian cricket deceives the ear. By altering the volume of its song, it can throw its voice like a ventriloquist. The sound appears to come from different points. Enemies can not get a bearing on the sound and then find it almost impossible to locate the insect.

IN THE SHADOWS

Good camouflage involves behaviour as well as colour. No matter how perfect an animal's colouring may be, shadows on the ground or a sudden movement can still lead to discovery. Most camouflage is useless if the animal moves around; so a camouflaged animal generally remains absolutely motionless in times of danger.

Shadows are a problem, particularly for animals that live on flat, open ground. In most cases an animal conceals its shadow by crouching or by flattening itself. When hiding, a deer crouches with its head and neck along the ground. This reduces its shadow. Its spotted coat then blends into sun-speckled vegetation. Some animals, in particular fish, have developed a flattened shape to aid concealment. Shadows can also be reduced by the way an animal places itself in relation to the Sun. Butterflies first close their wings above their back and then land facing the Sun. Their shadow is then just a thin line.

The caterpillar of a geometrid moth exactly matches the leaf it feeds on.

DRESSED CRABS

Some animals, particularly marine animals, make their own disguises. The Mediterranean masking crab (*Inachus scorpio*) is one such animal which, with great care, 'dresses' itself according to its surroundings. The crab takes a piece of seaweed and tears it like paper. Having chewed one end, possibly to soften it, the crab then attaches the seaweed to its body. The sponge crab (genus *Dromia*) disguises itself by holding a piece of sponge above its back with hind legs which have been adapted for this purpose. The sponge eventually begins to grow on the crab's shell. Yet another crab *(Dorippe astuta)*, holds a leaf above its back to escape detection.

Walking leaf

Many insects resemble leaves. But perhaps the most perfect is the Indonesian leaf insect (genus *Phyllium*). With paper-thin wings and a ragged body, it looks just like a cluster of the half-eaten leaves that it lives among. It walks very slowly, swaying slightly like leaves in a breeze, and so makes the disguise even more effective. The insect's disguise is so good that other leaf-eating insects have been known to take a bite out of it.

BIRDS WITH BLACK EGGS

Some birds, such as the plover, ptarmigan, and nightjar, nest on the ground in open country. So their eggs are in constant danger from predators. Camouflage is essential. There are two ways of protecting the eggs. These can be coloured so that they match their surroundings. A striking example of this is an African bird, Temminck's courser. Its eggs are almost black, and the bird lays them among the black droppings of antelopes. Plovers and oystercatchers are other birds whose eggs are camouflaged. But sometimes the bird, rather than its eggs, is camouflaged. The female willow ptarmigan (*Lagopus lagopus*) is camouflaged with a mottled summer plumage of brown, grey, and yellow. Lying closely on the nest, neither hen nor eggs can be seen. The male is very conspicuous, keeping its white winter plumage until well after the young are hatched. Then it changes to its summer colouring. It is thought that in this way the male can distract predators from the nesting hen.

The chameleon prawn (*Hippolyte varians*) changes colour every night to a brilliant blue. During the day its colour matches the seaweed where it lives. If it moves to another weed, within a week its colour will match its new home. The prawn changes colour by means of hormones that regulate the flow of different pigments from its pigment cells.

COLOUR CONSCIOUS

Of all animals that change colour to match their surroundings, the chameleon is probably the best known. Its skin contains black, yellow, and red colour cells called chromatophores. They look something like stars with branches. Each cell contains pigment (colouring matter). There are also whitish cells which can scatter light to produce bluish colour. The black pigment can be made to spread out over a large area, or reduced to a tiny point. The cell branches also expand or contract, which helps to distribute the pigment. Nerve impulses pass information about the colour and pattern of its background from the chameleon's eye to its brain which sends out signals to activate the colour cells. For example, if the background is reddish in colour, the black cells will contract. The chameleon's skin becomes reddish because the red pigments show through.

Strange Partnerships

There are many unlikely partnerships in the animal world. They are often brought about by the need for defence or the search for food. Sometimes both partners benefit, sometimes only one—and sometimes one is actually harmed. One partnership may lead to another; there are many cases where a large animal's parasites are eaten by a smaller one.

LIVING TOGETHER

The general name for animal partnerships is symbiosis, from the Greek words *syn*, 'with' and *bios*, 'live'. There are three main kinds of symbiosis.

Below: Egyptian plovers feed by picking parasites from Nile crocodiles—even from between their teeth.

Mutualism benefits both partners. An example is the way hermit crabs often carry sea anemones on their borrowed shells. The sea anemone receives free transport and some food while the crab is protected by its passenger's stinging cells.

Commensalism is a more one-sided arrangement, in which the host animal provides shelter or transport for its 'guest' but gets nothing in return. Insects live in the nests of small rodents, such as mice, while some mice live in the houses of Man.

Parasitism is also a one-sided arrangement, in which the host is actually harmed by its guests. Tapeworms and flukes, which live inside mammals, can cause great damage to their hosts. Even external parasites such as fleas and lice can cause harm by transmitting disease to the host.

The cuckoo swops one of its eggs for that of another bird, and leaves an unwitting foster parent to hatch the chick. When the cuckoo is born, it heaves any other tenants out of the nest, and continues to be fed by its foster parent.

BITERS BITTEN

Great fleas have lesser fleas
Upon their backs to bite 'em;
The lesser fleas have smaller fleas,
And so ad infinitum.

This old rhyme is indeed true. For example, mites have been found on a cat's fleas. But most cases of parasitism are simpler. There are two principal kinds of parasites.

External parasites like fleas and lice live on the outside of a host animal, often by sucking their host's blood. Some are the larvae of independent creatures like warble flies. The fly lays its eggs on the skin of a cow or horse, and when they hatch, the larvae burrow into its flesh and feed on its blood. The larva under the skin causes a small swelling called a warble, with an air hole to allow the larva to breathe. When the larvae are ready to turn into pupae they drop to the ground.

Internal parasites, like tapeworms, trichina worms, and hookworms, live inside an animal, usually in its digestive system. Many infect Man. Such parasites can cause severe illness in the host.

The male deep-sea angler-fish *(Photocorynus spiniceps)* is a parasite on the female. Minute in comparison, he is attached to her skin and lives on her blood. Even more bizarre is the roundworm *Trichosomoides crassicauda*. The female is a tiny parasite in a rat's bladder—and the male is smaller still and lives inside the female!

HOUSEHOLD HARMONY

Once a hermit crab has moved into the discarded shell of a large mollusc, other lodgers soon follow. The soft-bodied crab uses the shell as armour against predators. One of the largest hermit crabs, *Pangurus bernhardus*, deliberately places a sea anemone on the outside of the shell, taking advantage of its stinging cells for its own protection. When the crab grows and has to move to a larger shell, it takes the anemone with it. Inside the shell, along with the crab, there is often another lodger, the ragworm *Nereis fucata*. It apparently lives on minute organisms that grow on the crab's body.

SWEET ALLIANCE

A fruitful partnership exists between the honey badger, or ratel *(Mellivora capensis)* and the honeyguides, small birds in the family Indicatoridae which live in tropical Africa. The birds like to eat the wax and larvae of wild bees but cannot open their nests and are afraid of their stings. So, when a honeyguide finds a bees' nest, it leads a ratel there. The ratel, whose thick fur protects it from stinging, breaks open the nest to get at the honey. The honeyguides feast on the remains.

Above: African oxpeckers perch on the back of a Cape buffalo, ridding it of ticks and insects. In return for providing the oxpeckers with food, the mammal is warned of danger by the birds' alarm calls.

CLEANER FISH

Wrasses of the genus *Labroides*, which live in the waters of the Pacific and Indian oceans, make their living as valets. They eat parasites like fish lice off the bodies of larger fish—and the service is much appreciated. They even enter the mouths of voracious fish that would normally make an appetiser of any fish so small. The cleaner fish maintain 'cleaning stations' which the larger fish visit to have parasites removed.

The wrasses are not the only valet fishes of the seas. Cleaner and barber fishes belong to many orders and families of fishes.

The peacock's spectacular display seems to
have little effect on the hens, but mating does take
place eventually.

Finding a Mate

Many invertebrate animals are asexual, that is, they can reproduce themselves individually by one means or another. But higher animals, including all vertebrates, reproduce sexually: they require a mate.

Animals that spend their time in herds or flocks, such as antelopes or seagulls, have no difficulty in finding a mate, though there may be fierce competition among males—which is why you see stags fighting. But some animals lead such solitary lives that it is a wonder they ever find a mate at all. Some moths signal to each other by smell, fireflies glow brightly, and crickets make chirping noises.

Once the chosen mate has been found the problem really begins for the male of the species. Will she, won't she . . . and the males use a great many different ways of luring their intended spouses. Some rely on display. Birds in particular do this. The male is generally much more brightly coloured than the female, and he struts in front of her, displaying his colours and dancing about. The peacock's brilliant display is far the most beautiful of all such wooing by colour. Some animals take a gift to the female. Jackdaws and other birds have been known to take gifts of food, and a male penguin rolls a stone towards the female—presumably to make her think of eggs! But some animals, such as the elephant, do all their wooing in secret, and little is known about it.

Above: The male Fighting fish (blue) wraps itself around the female to mate.

The male Adelie penguin offers a female a pebble. If she accepts, they build a nest of stones together.

207

Animal Homes

Many animals, such as beavers, rabbits and bees, build elaborate permanent homes, Others, such as cats and birds, build temporary nests in which to have their young. Birds are the most famous nest-builders. Their nests range in size and complexity from mere hollows in the ground and small heaps of sticks to the nests of the Australian bower bird, which take weeks or months to construct. But not all birds make nests – king penguins, for example, which live in the Antarctic, would be unable to find materials to build a nest in their icy, barren homeland. These birds incubate their eggs by holding them off the cold ground with their feet, against the warmth of their own bodies.

A bird's territory—the area that it defends against rivals, and in which it sings to advertise its presence—extends some distance on all sides of the nest. For example, you will rarely find more than one cock robin in a garden—if you do, they will be fighting savagely!

A VARIETY OF NESTS

There is no housing-estate monotony in the bird world—nests come in as many different shapes and styles as you can imagine.

Leaves stitched together with plant fibres make nests for tailorbirds (genus *Orthotomus*).

Burrows in the ground are used as nests by puffins (*Fratercula arctica*) and burrowing owls (*Speotyto cunicularia*).

Holes in trees are home for many kinds of owls, and particularly for woodpeckers (family Picidae), which excavate their own with their chisel-like beaks.

Mud is the main ingredient for nests made by swifts (family Apodidae) and swallows and martins (Hirundinidae). They use their saliva as cement—and the edible-nest swiftlet (*Collocalia inexpectata*) makes its nest from saliva alone.

Hollows in the ground, barely deep enough to prevent the eggs from rolling away, provide 'home' for many gulls (family Laridae).

Twigs form the basis of a nest for a stork (family Ciconiidae)—plus mud, straw, rags and anything else to make a home that may be 8 feet (2.4 m) across!

The Golden oriole (1) suspends its nest from the branches. The Great horned owl (2) takes over abandoned nests. The tailorbird (3) sews leaves together. The baya weaver (4) builds a nest near the rest of its community. The Ruby-throated hummingbird (5) has a delicate, round nest. The long-tailed tit (6) builds a domed nest.

IT'S HOME
Badger: Earth or set.
Beaver: Lodge
Fox: Earth or kennel
Hare: Form
Lion and bear: Den
Otter: Holt
Rabbit: Burrow or warren
Squirrel: Drey

A beaver's lodge.
Beavers select a stretch of river to build on, and dam the river if the water is too shallow. The dam is usually about 4 feet (1.2 m) high and may be up to 300 feet (90 m) long. The living chamber is above water level and is reached through tunnels with underwater entrances.

Below: Lemmings nose about in and above the tunnels of their colony. These smallish rodents are most famous for their migrations, which sometimes lead to mass drownings when they come to a body of water.

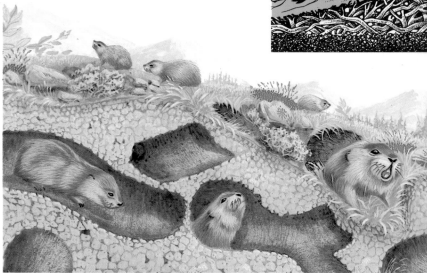

HOUSEPROUD BADGERS
Badgers (*Meles meles*) and their American cousins (*Taxidea taxus*) are among the most houseproud of animals. They dig long, rambling tunnels into a woodland bank, with living quarters lined with dried grass. No rubbish is allowed in this 'set'—it is all taken out and dumped well away from the home. The badgers dig themselves latrines a little way from the set's entrance.

211

INSECT COLONIES

Some insects form regular colonies or settlements. Bees do this and so do ants. As with bees, there are three kinds of ants—queens, laying eggs; males who do not work; and a corps of female workers. An ant colony contains a great many cells or chambers, with different purposes. The queen lives in one, laying eggs. Next door is the hatching room, from which the grubs as they turn into pupae are carried into another room to develop.

The ants construct other rooms for special purposes, such as storing food—seeds and grains—rearing fungus on which to feed, or keeping aphids (family Aphididae). The aphids are 'milked' like cows. An ant colony may contain several queens, each with its own suite of rooms.

HOUSES OF SAND

The lugworm (*Arenicola marina*), much prized by fishermen for bait, lives in an L-shaped burrow in the sand. It swallows a mixture of sand and organic matter, digests the food, and passes the sand out to form casts on the surface.

Some shore-living worms, like the sand mason (*Lanice conchilega*), build tubes of grains of sand, cemented together. The animal lives inside the tube, with its tentacles waving out of the end. Many sea-urchins, such as the sea potato or sand urchin (*Echinocardium cordatum*), make burrows in the sand, with long funnels leading up to the surface. Another, a kind of purple sea-urchin (*Paracentrotus lividus*), makes its burrow in a crack in solid rock—and when it grows cannot escape through the narrow opening.

Above: The mason worm builds a home out of grains of sand glued together with a secreted fluid.

212

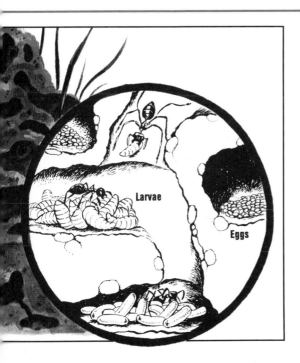

Highest home is probably that of the pika (genus *Ochotowa*), a small mammal related to the rabbit; it lives in the high Himalaya mountains. Pikas have been found at heights of up to 17,500 feet (5,300m) above sea level.

Most mobile homes are probably those made by tree swallows (*Iridoprocne bicolor*) on ferry boats plying on the St Lawrence River.

Strangest nest was probably one made by a sparrow (*Passer domesticus*) in Switzerland, which consisted entirely of watch springs!

Largest nest is that built by Sociable weavers (*Philetairus socius*) of south-western Africa, a structure several yards across housing hundreds of birds in separate chambers.

Looking After Young

Above: The male Three-spined stickleback builds a nest for the female to lay her eggs in, then guards it until the eggs hatch. Male sea-horses and pipefishes carry the eggs in their brood pouches.

Most fish lay their eggs and take no further interest in their young. Elephants, on the other hand, take care of their calves for several years after birth. Animals that do not protect their young themselves generally lay large numbers of eggs. The ocean sunfish (*Mola mola*) lays up to 300,000,000 eggs at a time. The oceans would be unable to contain these fish, which can be more than 10 feet (3 m) long, if they all survived. But most of them fall victim to predators.

Animals that do take care of their young produce far fewer of them, sometimes only one every one or two years. Parental care is highest among the mammals, which suckle their young. Most parent birds also work hard to feed their young until they are old enough to forage for themselves.

SEA CUCUMBERS

Even some of the simplest organisms exercise some kind of care over their offspring. The female sea-cucumber of the genus *Synapta*, like other sea-cucumbers, lays eggs in the sea where they are fertilized by the sperm of the male. The eggs in due course hatch into a free-swimming form known as *auriculariae*. But with some species, the mother puts her eggs in pockets in the skin, and keeps the hatchlings with her for a considerable time.

Most amphibians lay their eggs in water and leave them. But the male midwife toad carries the eggs in strings around his legs until they hatch.

If you turn a female brook leech (*Glossiphonia complanata*) upside down during the breeding season you will find either the eggs stuck to her belly, or else the baby leeches, each holding on with its sucker. This helps to prevent the young from being washed away by the swift current of the streams where these leeches live.

Above: a foal suckles from its dam, and below, a swallow returns from foraging insects to feed its hungry brood.

BIRDS AS PARENTS

Parental duties among most birds are taken very seriously and mean hard work for both parents. Among birds living in harems, such as domestic fowls (*Gallus gallus*), the male takes little part in rearing the young. A large number of birds are monogamous—they have only one mate; some birds, like jackdaws (*Corvus monedula*) and birds of prey such as the osprey (*Pandion haliaëtus*) apparently mate for life. The cock bird takes an equal part with the female in building the nest, and in fetching food for the young when they hatch. In some species, such as king penguins (*Aptenodytes patagonica*), both parents share the task of incubating the solitary egg.

Instinct and Learning

Many animals are born into the world with well-developed patterns of behaviour — such as the one shown by the chick in the picture below. This kind of behaviour and knowledge is said to be instinctual. Other kinds of behaviour and knowledge have to be learned. Most examples of behaviour among higher animals are really a mixture of the two.

For example, a kitten learns hunting techniques through play with its mother and fellow kittens — but its instinct tells it to hunt, without any prompting.

It is true to say that the behaviour of lower animals is mostly instinctual and stereotyped — yet even a lowly flatworm can be taught, by electric shocks, to swim in a pre-arranged path.

IMPRINTING

During the first few minutes, sometimes a longer period, of a baby bird's life a curious process known as *imprinting* takes place. Experiments with geese and ducks carried out by Dr Konrad Lorenz and others showed that within a few hours of hatching, a duckling or gosling knows the colouring, outline, and voice of its parent. From then on it will follow its mother everywhere, and copy her actions. Later on in its life the bird will also congregate with members of its own species.

Dr Lorenz discovered that if the chicks are taken away from their mother and spend those first few vital hours with a foster-parent, they will become imprinted on the foster-parent. He and his helpers found themselves acting as foster-parents to greylag geese, who ignored their own kind and followed the humans everywhere. These birds later proved to be psychologically incapable of mating with their own kind.

Wolves learn their hunting techniques from their elders. When hunting such large prey as caribou, wolves need to cooperate closely with one another, to separate the kill —usually a weakly or immature animal — from the rest of the herd.

A chick, on the other hand, does not need to learn to crouch and freeze when a bird of prey flies over: this crouching is instinctive. However, the young bird does learn later on that crouching is unnecessary when a harmless large bird, such as a swan, flies overhead.

217

A cheetah kitten plays with its mother's tail. All members of the cat family play when young. Their play is related to hunting, and in fact is a type of learning.

STIMULUS AND RESPONSE

When an animal shows instinctual behaviour, it does so in response to a trigger or stimulus. This stimulus, or 'releaser' — so-called because it releases behaviour–can be anything that affects the animal's senses in a special way. An example of a releaser is the first sight, to a newly hatched duckling, of its mother.

Hearing as well as sight can release behaviour in birds. Hen budgerigars will not mate or lay eggs until they hear the soft warble of the cock bird. He also has a loud warble, which stimulates the secretion of hormones into his own blood. Hormones determine each phase, or stage, of their sexual behaviour. Many birds have a long and complicated courtship, which may involve special dances or feather displays. Each stage of a display is controlled by the secretion of hormones, and brings mating a little closer.

The behaviour of birds is under very close hormone control, and so is mostly instinctual.

But of course, even our own sexual behaviour follows an instinctual pattern of stimulus and response. Other patterns of instinctual behaviour that we share with animals include the responses of rage and fear — we do not *tell* our heart to pound or the hairs on our head to stand upright.

Baby monkeys cling to their mothers instinctively, as they are carried through the trees. This baby monkey clings rather pathetically to a cloth-covered artificial mother.

Hibernation

Hibernation—the winter sleep—is one of the great puzzles of the animal world. In northern parts of the world, winter is a time of food shortage. Some animals deal with this problem by migrating—many birds do this. Others forage harder, eat less, sleep more, and generally battle through the winter in very much their normal way.

But a few animals indulge in a complete change of life during winter. They include some rodents such as dormice, Prairie dogs, and marmots; bats; and insectivores such as hedgehogs. Some reptiles, toads and frogs also indulge in a form of hibernation. Other animals such as bears spend much of the winter sleeping, but in an incomplete form of hibernation. Most hibernating animals wake up if the weather turns warm, and look round for something to eat.

A BUILT-IN HOT WATER BOTTLE

Brown fat is one of the secrets of hibernation. This substance contains many more droplets of fat than the ordinary white fat found in most mammals, so providing a much richer store for the animal to draw on.

All new-born animals—including human babies—have brown fat in their bodies, but most of them lose it as they grow older. The hibernating animals keep it. It acts as a built-in hot water bottle, and in babies and young animals keeps them warm until they are old enough to be able to shiver—shivering is another process that Nature has provided to produce heat!

House mice are known to flourish in cold stores, where an ordinary animal would die of the cold. The secret: brown fat again. The animals have a reserve store of heat which keeps them alive and well.

The long sleep:
1. Snake 2. bear
3. woodchuck
4. toad
5. lizard

220

The brown fat store is drawn on by order of the *hypothalamus*, which is the temperature-regulating part of the brain. When hibernation ends the hypothalamus draws heavily on the fat—so an animal can go from as low a temperature as 10°C (50°F) to 37°C (99°F) in a few hours.

THE MECHANISM OF HIBERNATION

Hibernation is more than just a deep sleep. The hibernating animal's rate of breathing and its pulse speed both slow down, as in sleep but to a greater degree. But the body temperature also drops considerably—often to around 10°C (50°F).

In this condition the whole body metabolism is running in slow gear. The heart beats incredibly slowly, and the digestion is just ticking over. A hibernating animal starts the winter very fat, and this store of fat is drawn on to supply the body's needs during the long sleep. Some animals such as mice and squirrels make a cache of nuts and other food which they can draw on during the winter, and these animals do not sleep so long or so soundly as the true hibernators.

The animals that do best in hibernation are those that can curl up in a well-insulated nest, like the dormouse. For if the temperature around the animal falls too low, the stores of fat are burned up too quickly and the animal dies.

Right: More hibernating animals: 1. dormouse; 2. hedgehog; 3. tortoise; 4. squirrel.

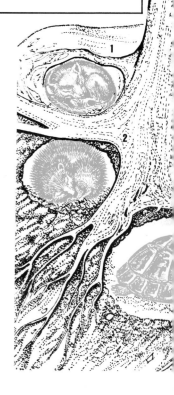

A horshoe bat hibernates, hanging upside down, in the darkness of a cave.

THE WINTERING SNAIL

Land snails (order Stylommatophora) have their own form of winter sleep in temperate or colder climates. Before the onset of winter the snail slows down (if that seems possible) and starts looking around for winter quarters. It buries itself in some sheltered spot, covered by moss or soil. Then it withdraws into its shell and shuts the door.

The 'door' is a special cold-weather lid, known as the *epiphragm*, which the snail makes from a mixture of mucus, calcium carbonate, and phosphate. It secretes this mixture, similar to that which forms its shell, from part of the body called the mantle. The snail leaves a tiny gap to allow a minimum of oxygen to enter from the outer air, and so keep the body's functions ticking over.

SUMMER HIBERNATION

Hot and very dry weather can also send some animals to sleep. They retreat into a sheltered spot in order to slumber through a drought, which could be as killing as a severe winter. Among the animals that go through this process of *aestivation* (summer sleep) are snails, and reptiles such as crocodiles and snakes. The African lungfish burrows in the mud of its dried up rivers and waits for the waters to flow again.

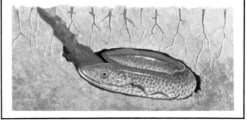

Navigation

How do animals find their way about? For navigating routes, and hunting down prey, all animals rely on senses such as vision, hearing and smell, but the importance of these varies widely in animals of different groups.

Invertebrate animals rely very largely on their senses of smell and taste. The smell-taste organs of flies are located on the feet. Some invertebrates, however, such as dragonflies and octopuses, have highly developed eyes, and hunt mostly by sight.

Among the lower vertebrates, sharks detect and follow their prey by smell, until at very close range they home in for the kill using their vision. But even such an advanced vertebrate as the wolf needs its nose to track its prey: its sense of smell is far better than our own. Other animals which have highly developed senses include bats and dolphins, which can hear sounds so high-pitched they are inaudible to other animals.

Some animals rely heavily on senses that are completely unfamiliar to us. A fish such as a herring, swimming together with all the others, keeps its position in the shoal mainly by means of a sense organ called the lateral line system, which detects the position of vibrations in the water. Some other fishes have special electric organs that help the fishes to find their way about in muddy waters.

Bats send out very high-pitched sounds through their mouths or noses. The sounds bounce off objects, such as branches or insects, in their flight path. By listening to the echoes of these sounds a bat can judge how far away an obstacle is. Under a test, a bat has flown for hours among a tangle of wires without touching one. The inset picture shows how bats can dive and turn quickly to capture insect food.

Incredible Journeys

Sunshine all year round is the dream of many people—a dream they will never realize. Yet many animals manage it by migration. Every summer birds nest and bring up their young in the temperate regions of Europe and North America, where there are plenty of insects and seeds for them to eat. Then as the colder weather approaches and the food supply begins to dwindle they set off on the long flight to southern climes.

Some of the more important migration routes used by birds. Most prefer to keep close to land.

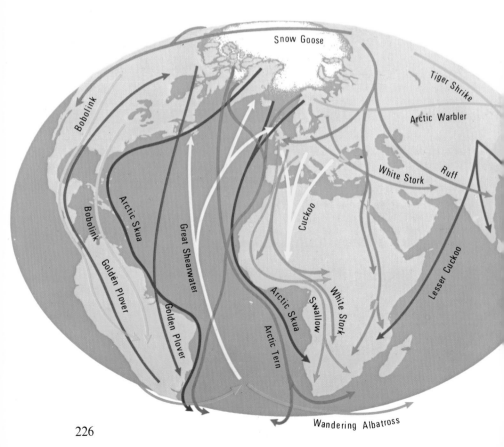

Snow Goose

Tiger Shrike

Arctic Warbler

Bobolink

White Stork

Ruff

Bobolink

Arctic Skua

Great Shearwater

Cuckoo

Golden Plover

Arctic Skua

Swallow

White Stork

Lesser Cuckoo

Golden Plover

Arctic Tern

Wandering Albatross

FLYING TO THE GOOD LIFE

Every spring millions of birds migrate from their winter quarters to the temperate regions of the world to breed. These regions abound with food on which the parents can rear their hungry chicks.

The biggest migrations are to the northerly parts of North America, Europe, and Asia. But there is some migration to the southern hemisphere. For example, the double-banded dotterel flies from Australia to New Zealand to breed—a journey of 1,400 miles (2,250 km). The American golden plover (*Pluvialis dominica*) does a non-stop flight of 2,065 miles (3,323 km) between Alaska and Hawaii.

Migration is mainly triggered off by changes in the length of the day, which cause a change in the bird's hormone balance. The bird eats more and becomes increasingly restless. There is evidence that birds use the Sun and stars to navigate by, because when the sky is cloudy, they often become hopelessly lost.

Migrating birds fly at many different heights. Some skim over the ground or the waves. Waders—a group including dotterels, avocets, and plovers—fly at between 3,000 feet and 6,000 feet (900 m—1800 m). Birds fly much higher when crossing mountains, and geese have been seen in the Himalayas at almost 29,500 feet (9,000 m) above sea level.

Ornithologists have tracked the annual migration of the Slender-tailed shearwater (*Puffinus tenuirostris*). These amazing birds, no more than 20 inches (50 cm) long, travel right round the Pacific Ocean. They breed on islands between Australia and Tasmania. In April millions of them set off north across the Coral Sea and up to the Sea of Japan. By June they are crossing the Bering Sea, to fly south down the Pacific coast of Canada. They then fly back to Tasmania by way of Hawaii and Fiji, arriving at the breeding grounds always on September 26 and 27.

The land crab (*Geoarcoidea humei*) of the Malacca Strait spends part of its life scavenging in the forests, then makes for the shore to spawn. The adults then return to the forest, while the young crabs hatch in the sea. They then make the journey inland. Their gills can breathe in air.

Locusts do not migrate every year—but when they do they travel in vast swarms which can obscure sunlight. When they land, they do dreadful damage to crops.

227

THE MYSTERIOUS EEL
In the Sargasso Sea, a region of still waters full of densely floating seaweed between the West Indies and the Azores, is the breeding ground of the eel (genus *Anguilla*). The tiny larvae—about 3 inches (8 cm) long—drift with the ocean currents, some to North America, others to Europe. The European eels spend three years on the journey and then travel far inland up rivers, where they stay up to nine years. They then return to the sea and begin their 3,000-mile (4,800-km) swim back to the breeding grounds of the Sargasso Sea—and that without eating!

A salmon struggles up a rocky stream as it returns to spawn in the river in which it was born. The young may travel 1,000 miles (1,600 km) from the river mouth, but they will always return.

228

Left: the Arctic tern, which holds the record for migration.

ON THE TRAIL OF THE CARIBOU

The caribou (*Rangifer arcticus*) of Alaska are among the few mammals that migrate. They winter in the woodland areas south of the Brooks Range of mountains. In spring the pregnant cows wander northwards to the tundra, the region of winter ice and summer vegetation bordering the Arctic Ocean. There they have their calves. The bulls follow the cows north, but mate only when the herd has returned to the southern woodlands.

JOURNEY'S END

Longest bird migration is by the Arctic tern (*Sterna paradisaea*), which leads a life of perpetual summer. It leaves the Arctic as summer ends and flies 11,000 miles (18,000 km) to Antarctica. At the end of the Antarctic summer it flies back to its breeding ground—so making a round trip of 22,000 miles (36,000 km).

Longest mammal migration is by the Alaska seal (*Callorhinus ursinus*), which does a round trip of 6,000 miles (9,600 km).

Most travelled butterfly is the monarch butterfly (*Danaus plexippus*) of North America, which migrates 2,500 miles (4,000 km) from Hudson Bay to Florida and back.

Index

Index

Index

Index